PS
374
.I7
B6
1976
cop.1

Bolger, Stephen
  Garrett.

The Irish character
  in American
  fiction, 1830-1860

$19.00 R0065414688

© THE BAKER & TAYLOR CO.

THE IRISH-AMERICANS

THE IRISH CHARACTER IN AMERICAN FICTION, 1830-1860

Stephen Garrett Bolger

ARNO PRESS

A New York Times Company

New York — 1976

Editorial Supervision: ANDREA HICKS

———◆———

First publication in book form, 1976,
   by Arno Press, Inc.
Copyright © 1971 by Stephen Garrett Bolger

THE IRISH-AMERICANS
ISBN for complete set: 0-405-09317-9
See last pages of this volume for titles.

Manufactured in the United States of America

———◆———

Library of Congress Cataloging in Publication Data

Bolger, Stephen Garrett.
   The Irish character in American fiction, 1830-1860.

   (The Irish-Americans)
   Reprint of the author's thesis, University of Pennsyl-
vania.
   1. American fiction--19th century--History and
criticism. 2. Irish in literature. I. Title.
II. Series.
PS374.I7B6 1976   813'.3'09352   76-6323
ISBN 0-405-09320-9

THE IRISH CHARACTER IN AMERICAN FICTION, 1830-1860

Stephen Garrett Bolger

A DISSERTATION

in

American Civilization

Presented to the Faculty of the Graduate School of Arts
and Sciences of the University of Pennsylvania in
Partial Fulfillment of the Requirements for the
Degree of Doctor of Philosophy

1971

_____
Supervisor of Dissertation

_____
Graduate Group Chairman

PREFACE

The subject of this study is not the relation between fact and fiction, although that relation is necessarily raised. The subject rather is the fiction in fiction; in other words, it is the pre-existing conventional character of the Irishman, drawn from other literary works and passed on to later writers to use in their turn. This study is not, therefore, a contribution to the history of immigration. It is an attempt to define and describe the Irish image as part of the furniture of the American mind. This image needs the background of history to make its nature clear, but it reveals more about the people who hold and use it than it does about that historical background.

A word should be said about the fiction used for a sample. The method adopted in this study is the analysis of a random sample of American works, to the end that the investigator's presuppositions will not affect the presuppositions buried in the fiction. One immediate consequence of this method is that major authors and major works occupy a small place in the sample. Readers should note that the subject of the study is not precisely literature either, and that the image of the Irishman is conceived as a common intellectual concept in the society, to be defined from its separate appearances in many works.

iii

I. INTRODUCTION

This study is an examination of those characters who
can be identified as Irish in a sample of American fiction published in the years 1830 to 1860. It proposes to
describe the range of character traits, behavior, status
and role attributed to these characters; that is, to
describe the convention of the Irish character. It will
also examine the implications of this convention for the
assimilation of the Irish character into the American
imagination.

The chosen period offers good prospects for apprais-
ing the literature itself and the Irish character in the
literature. Since these years span the large Irish immigration of the 1840's, the ten years before may be
expected to provide a view of American images of the Irish
before the mass immigration presented a social problem.
Though the whole population of America was the product of
immigration, and though immigration had never stopped,
no group before had come so poor, so identified as a mass;
no group had ever concentrated itself so exclusively in
cities. Furthermore, the Irish met an increasingly organized religious hostility. They thus may have provoked
a reassessment of the images of Irishness held by

Americans. The period covers the decade of the 1850's,
through the peak of immigration and past it to the brink
of Civil War, when other issues overrode nativism.

In literature, too, this period covers the first
great outpouring of American fiction, a flowering both in
numbers and in quality. Before 1830 there were no more
than twenty titles of fiction by Americans published in
America in any single year. The numbers rose sharply
after 1830. From 1830 to 1839 the annual average was
35 titles; in the '40's the average was 94, and in
the '50's, over 125.[1] The total number of separate
titles published from 1830 to 1860 is just under 2,700;
the number published before 1830 is less than 250. Contemporary changes in printing and distribution brought
alterations in the format of books and the price of publi-
cations as well. Cheap paperback novels proliferated at
the same time as Poe, Hawthorne, and Melville were writing.
Both good fiction and cheap fiction multiplied, and by
inference the audience grew and changed also.

Fiction as Source

Fiction offers the student of history a rich deposit
of manners and attitudes, judgements on contemporary

---

[1]The figures in this section are from Lyle H. Wright,
American Fiction; 1774-1850: A Contribution Toward A
Bibliography. Revised Edition (San Marino, 1948) and
American Fiction, 1851-1875: A Contribution Toward A
Bibliography (San Marino, 1957).

events, and descriptions of classes and institutions.
But it gives these in the context of an arbitrary construction, so that there is no way to judge how much of
the material is reliable as an indication of contemporary
reality, without verifying it through historical investi-
gation. As a source for history, fiction can only be
used after it has been independently shown to be accurate.

Though fiction is useful, if limited, in adding
depth to political and social history, this study aims to
use literature as its primary source. The problem then
presents itself: where can we find a basis in the fiction
itself for direct and independent judgments about the
period?

The author of fiction may select his material in any
way that fits his purpose, and may arrange it as he will
for his effects. He is free to create biased characters,
or to inject his own view at any point. This virtually
unlimited freedom to manipulate and distort reality makes
the author a poor source for fact.

But his freedom is not entirely without bounds. He
is limited most obviously by the requirements of the
language. He must choose words within meanings determined by usage, or fail to be understood. He is obliged
to refer to the set of expectations about words which he
shares with his audience. It should be clear that he

does not submit to the audience externally as judge; rather he refers to his own concept of the language. He writes out of his possession of the norms of language; grammar, syntax, meaning. The completeness and flexibility of a writer's grasp of what is possible in his language is the major determinant of his quality.

The system of language, internalized in the process of growing up as a personal disposition, is one limit which ties the author to a social context. Take the position a step further: the author also knows, from his past experience with his form, how stories proceed. He knows what characters are possible, and which will suit his need; he knows actions and their significance. This knowledge is also the result of his social experience, and he shares this too with his audience, as products of a common environment.

The expectations about character and action which are shared by the writer and his audience are literary conventions. The Irish character is a literary convention. The purpose of this study is to discover the shared expectations of authors and readers concerning this specific element in the fiction. It is the reaching into the audience by way of convention that will enable direct judgments to be made about the American imagination of the period.

Conventions of Character

A character type or convention is a set of expected qualities and behavior patterns. Such types occur in literature of all ages. Falstaff as the braggart, Hamlet as the melancholy man, appear in the plays initially as characters whose tastes, motivation, and possible behavior are understood by the audience. From the initial appearance, certain things are allowed to the character, and certain other things are nearly impossible. The types save time in starting the work, an important consideration in the brief span available to the dramatist; but their use is equally common in fiction. Conventional images are available--and often nearly inescapable--for Negroes, sheriffs, mothers-in-law. An author who names his characters in these ways automatically invokes responses from his audience.

The author is to some degree the prisoner of the image thus invoked; but he can in the course of the work free his character from the type. Such an alteration or refutation of the type may be the point of the work. Huckleberry Finn works such a change in Jim. Jim begins as a stock Negro slave: irresponsible, superstitious, shuffling, dependent. All of these traits are reversed through the adventures he encounters--though Twain reverts to the stock character in comic set-pieces and at the conclusion.

The point is that the initial understanding of Jim's character is conventional; it relies on common images well understood by writer and audience. That the book makes its social point through the destruction of this image suggests that the image itself is important socially, and needs correction. The stock, conventional Negro image produces reactions which block people from responding properly to reality; it is dangerous. The type manifests the mind of the audience blindly at odds with reality.

Conventions of character have importance, and have consequences. They also have a history. They may appear, alter, and disappear in response to changes in the public imagination. They may experience crises, in which conscious efforts are made to change them for social reasons. They may also persist in the face of such efforts despite the troubles they may cause. The image of the lazy, superstitious, obsequious darky, so beautifully broken in Jim, remained alive for another seventy-five years, through the plantation films of the 1930's. And Huck himself has reappeared in stories and on magazine covers in his original, conventional image, untouched by the personal growth and critical temper of Huck at the end of his own book. The work of correcting a simple image, a dangerous image, a comforting image, must be done over again so long as it seems necessary to do so.

The purpose of this study is to examine the qualities of the conventional Irish figure with these things in mind. If the Irishman is assumed to have a certain status, a predictable appearance, definite traits, these may lead to conclusions about his place in the American image of society.

Earlier Conventions of Irish Character

Because of the tendency of conventions to persist unchanged, we must examine the Irish convention at the point where it enters American fiction. J. O. Bartley has studied the national figures on the British stage from the earliest times to 1800, and his book offers a clear and useful sketch of the Irish figure.[2]

He notes the growth of an Irish convention in three stages: 1587-1659, 1660-1759, and 1760-1800. The first period does not concern us, since the figure is far from its later form and function.

In the second period the Irish character begins to take a form more like the later American character. Bogs and shillelaghs are common associations. The Irish are amorous and aggressive with women, often in pursuit of a fortune. They are bold and free in manners, often in

[2]J. O. Bartley, Teague, Shenkin and Sawney: Being an Historical Study of the Earliest Irish, Welsh and Scottish Characters in English Plays (Cork: Cork University Press, 1954).

fact impudent. They love to fight, regardless of the
cause, and they are courageous. They are not reliable
in the witness box. After 1700, the Irish character is
increasingly identified by blunders, and by that verbal
form of blunder known as the Irish bull. The bull is not
easy to define with precision. It has been said that the
point of an Irish bull is its pregnancy; one example often
given is that of the Irish legislator, urged to vote for
the good of posterity, who asked, "What has posterity
ever done for us?" Teague (spelled variously Teg, Tegue,
and Teigue) was the standard name for the Irishman around
1700; Teagueland was a popular equivalent for Ireland.[3]

By the period 1760-1800, the Irishman had become
thoroughly removed from reality, a "grossly exaggerated
and misleading" representation.[4] Bogs, bogtrotters, and
shillelaghs remain national emblems; to them are added
whiskey and music and the potato, now the sole food attributed to Ireland. The shamrock is little mentioned. It
had not yet become the symbol of national identity, and
was no longer the Irish national food, as it had been in
the seventeenth century.

---

[3]Probably from the continuing popularity of the character Teague in The Committee, by Sir Robert Howard, a
play which was revised and played through the eighteenth
century, rich in bulls and sentiment. Bartley, Teague,
pp. 102, 189.

[4]Bartley, Teague, p. 254.

The Irish character remained pugnacious and fero-
cious. The Irish were tall, strong and handsome; still
amorous and notable lovers, but not in this period
accused of fortune-hunting. Their manners are still free
and familiar, but not rude or offensive. The national
character is free, open, noble and liberal, and the Irish
are capable of honest sentiment. Their religion is
Catholic, but is mainly revealed in their oaths by saints
and the Virgin. There is very little hostility to them
on religious grounds.

Most Irish characters in this period are outside
Ireland, either in England or on the Continent. The principal occupations of Irish characters are servants, appearing in thirty-one plays; military officers, in twenty-four;
enlisted men, in sixteen, and laborers, who appear in
nineteen plays.[5] Since it was impossible (until the
Catholic Emancipation of 1829) for Catholics to hold a com-
mission in the British Army, British officers in the plays
are of Anglo-Irish families; Catholic Irish are officers
in the service of Continental armies.

---

[5]Bartley, Teague, p. 168. Of the laborers, six were
chair men, six were haymakers, five were porters, and two
were unemployed. Bartley notes that as Irish population
increased, Irish labor was driven to England as unskilled
labor and seasonal farm help, or into the army and navy
(p. 167). In this the plays conform to reality; but as
he also points out, the growing tensions in Irish life and
politics are completely ignored, smothered in sentimental
assumptions of Irish loyalty to England (pp. 166-167).

Conventional Irish speech is little developed, and Irish identification depends more on set phrases and a few key spellings than on careful imitation of actual Irish speech. (Brogue, formerly Irish footwear, now is applied to dialect). Common Irish indicators are such words as arrah, jewel, and honey; after used as a sign of tense (and often used incorrectly); and such phrases as a bit of a; at all, at all; and be easy (for be calm). Inversions, like "is it you now that are . . .", and progressives, like "may I be asking . . .", are also common ways of suggesting Irish dialect. Written indications of Irish pronunciation are few; the most common are represented by mane for mean and tunder for thunder.[6] In a play as performed these spellings would be filled out by the actor's full performance of the brogue (and many of the actors were Irish); but the very sparse written indications suggest that the authors were satisfied to touch only the most obviously conventional notes, and to let their reading audience fill in the image.

This English version of the Irish character is the point from which the American convention takes its start. It will serve as a preliminary set of expectations about character, role, and behavior. A high degree of conformity

_____

[6]Bartley, Teague, pp. 282-290, is a full treatment of Irish dialect and its history in the plays.

to this version of the Irish character will be taken to
indicate the persistence of the set pattern, the literary
image; as a sign that the traditional image obscures the
reality. Innovations and alterations in this character
will be taken as evidence of response of the image to the
pressure of contemporary events.

The Method of the Study

Every appearance of every character identified as
Irish[7] has been examined for indications of a possible
convention. Such indications include personal relationships to institutions and other people; personal characteristics, such as intemperance, appearance, names; occupations; roles in the plot; and speech.

Such relationships as religion and family ties are
important signs of stability or its opposite. Religion,
for the Irish, seems to cut both ways; strong religious
affiliation implies strong moral standards, but Catholic
affiliation may be a sign of dangerous political leanings.
A strong marriage or strong parent-child bonds are signs
of social stability; the absence of family is a mark of
instability and irresponsibility. Personal traits have

---

[7]In most cases it is impossible to distinguish
between newly immigrant Irish and those who have been in
the country for some time, or even between first and
second generation, because there is no evidence given.
The only criterion applied for inclusion of a character
as Irish is that he is marked as Irish by speech or by
observation.

obvious significance in the same direction when broadly
applied to a group.

The economic position and work performed by a character is also a good sign of his general relation to
others and to the social order. The representation of
many Irish as servants or unskilled labor is a mark of
the limits set to their social aspirations as a class.
If they do their work badly this is a further limitation.
Directly related to occupation is status, or the value put
on a character by others. The definition of status may be
through family, office held, or by mode of address. Other
characters may, of course, hold persons of low status in
high regard, and dislike those of high status.

Marks of the kind so far described are fairly easy
to identify objectively. Equally important, but far more
difficult to define clearly, is the function of a character within the imaginary world created in each work of
fiction. Many of the Irish characters in the fiction are
marginal in importance for the plot of the book or the
fate of its characters; a laborer passed in the street,
a maid who admits a visitor. Often Irish characters have
a purely indirect appearance in the work, as characters
in an anecdote told by a character actually in the story.
Though the characters of this kind are excellent testimony
to the convention of Irish character of the Pat-and-Mike

kind, they are not at all likely to show any relation to reality, and they are not really in the fiction.

The eligibility of any character to play a major or minor role in the world of the novel or story is probably the most important and informative sign of his position in the author's imagination. Under what circumstances can an Irishman be cast as the hero of a novel? To be the hero of most nineteenth century novels means to be eligible to marry the heroine. It is important to discover whether an Irish character can sustain this position. Another possible hero may be the center of an adventure story, a frontier tale, like Natty Bumppo. Do Irish appear in this kind of role? In fact, no Irish character is put into the role of either kind of hero in any novel, apart of course from some few books laid in Ireland with upper-class Irish characters. The thought of an Irish hero may violate probability for the American imagination; or it may offend against propriety; very possibly, it may not be at all interesting to author and audience. As we will see, it is possible to make Irish characters the heroes of short narratives, provoked by the problem of immigration and the urge to find a satisfactory resolution to this social problem. This interest was not sufficient to produce a novel.

Irish characters begin to appear in substantial

numbers in roles close to the center of plots but not
included in the main action. They do not marry, in the
novels of romance, or inherit, and they do not exercise
leadership in the adventure story. This degree of
importance--as confidant, body servant, loyal follower--
is apparently easy to imagine. Of course, the Irish character had filled these functions on the British stage,
so that the convention existed as model, though the
American labor supply may have reinforced the image. In
these roles Irish can be important, close to the great,
admirable in their qualities. This kind of attention
must be carefully appraised, however, since it may be
condescending, and may be a form of dismissal, an assumption that Irish are confined to inferior status. This
treatment of the Irish shows the same general characteristics as the conventional treatment of Indians and
Negroes. The same basic limitations on the roles they
play and the status they hold appear, though specific
roles and traits differ.

The sum of the personal traits, relationships, status, and roles of the Irish characters in the fiction of
the period is the Irish conventional character. From the
examination of this material will come an estimate of
the place this character holds in the American imagination.

The Selection of the Fiction

The written record of the American imagination in fiction is only a fraction of the material that once existed; those whose attitudes this study is looking for are dead, and their thoughts largely lost. But even this written record is too large to cope with in full. There are over 2,700 titles of fiction listed in Wright's volumes for the period 1830 to 1860. Some system is needed to select, from this massive total, a manageable number of titles.

One possibility is to select those books which treat the Irish at greatest length, or which focus on the problems of the Irish as their central concern. Such a selection would provide the greatest amount of useable material in the sample taken. It would also present the highest degree of conscious reflection and opinion on the Irish.

It would be very difficult, however, to find the proper books; titles are not a reliable guide to content, so that all the titles would have to be examined to determine the sample. But a more important objection is that these books would be likely to be partisan; they would be strongly pro- or anti- Irish. Furthermore, insofar as they were advancing arguments, they would be something other than fiction; they would be historical or political tracts. The imagery disclosed in this kind of sample

would be polarized, excessively articulate, and likely
to overstate the importance of the Irish and the feelings
aroused by them.

A second method of selecting a sample would take the
work of the best writers of the period--Hawthorne,
Melville, Poe--for the source of the study. This sample
would offer the insights of the best literary minds, those
most sensitive to images and their possibilities. Under
the best of circumstances, it would avoid the risk of
unintelligent repetitions of preconceived types, though
even distinguished writers do in fact frequently rely on
traditional images.

Unfortunately, the best of the novels and stories
show too little interest in the matter to provide a fair
bulk of evidence. In the six novels of Cooper read for
this study, for instance, there is in aggregate less than
two pages of material about the Irish. Whitman's Franklin
Evans presents an Irishman not one bit less conventional
in character or behavior than a dozen Irish in cheap paper
books. The Irish are simply not treated centrally in long
fictional forms; the material would be inadequate. Only
by progressive enlargement of the sample to include lesser
writers could a large enough body of material be obtained;
and the standard for the selection of these authors would
rapidly become arbitrary.

Most literary investigations have followed one or the other of these two methods of selection; if neither is satisfactory for the purpose of this study, a third method will be needed. The method chosen is random sampling of the total field of fiction.

Random sampling simply means that books are selected according to any consistent mathematical rule that insures even distribution of the titles selected through the total, without reference to type, content, or authorship. If a sample is random and large enough, it should resemble the group in qualities and attitudes. It will serve as a smaller substitute as a subject for analysis and description.

The size of the sample required depends on the variations expected in the group and the degree of accuracy desired. In sampling industrial products, for example, small samples are enough if experience with the items shows high consistency of quality. In fiction, variations may be expected to be very high, in subject matter and in attitudes; a safe sample will have to be quite large. Furthermore, though a fairly small sample would show the most common attitudes, this study cannot risk missing less common views. The sample chosen will have to be large, as samples are measured.

The great advantage of random sampling as the basis

for selection of a body of fiction is that it completely
eliminates the investigator's preconceptions and biases
as factors affecting the results. A study beginning in
this way escapes the difficult problem of representing
the output of the period fairly, without the interests
and tastes of the writer (in whatever direction they may
lie) affecting the conclusions by directing his choice of
material.

The Choice of The Sample

The basic problem in setting up a sampling method
for the fiction is to identify a universe; to discover
some list or collection which can be accepted as defining
the fiction produced in the period. The second step is
to arrive at a principle for selecting titles out of this
universe. The sample must be large enough; it should
ideally be reasonably accessible.

Lyle H. Wright's two volumes of American Fiction
were selected as the list defining the total body of fiction from 1830 to 1860. These lists are in the first
place confined to books written by Americans and published
in the United States; they are also confined to fiction--
as far as possible to adult fiction. Decisions on the
inclusion or exclusion of fiction-like materials--ficti-
tious biographies, sketches, travel books, and so forth--
have been made by the compiler. Equally useful is the

exclusion of juveniles, tracts, and so forth.[8] The
Wright lists, then, are as good a guide to the field of
adult American fiction in the period as can be found. In
addition, the books provide a finder list.

There is some risk in any list that it will not
include all the works actually published. An appendix to
the first volume of Wright lists seventy-three titles
gathered from publisher's announcements and other sources
which could not be located. Some of these were by well
known authors such as T. S. Arthur. Of course, some of
these may have been promised and never published (or published under another title). On the other hand, these
may be only a small part of the titles that have been
lost entirely. At any rate, the titles listed as lost in
Wright amount to less than five per cent of those listed
in the bibliography.

The next decision was to use those books held by the
library of the University of Pennsylvania as the first
selection of a sub-group for the sample. The possible
difficulties in this choice are first, whether the University holdings are adequate in size to represent a fair
cross-section, and whether there is reason to expect a
bias in the holdings that might affect the results.

If the acquisition policy of the library when these

---

[8]Wright, American Fiction, 1774-1850, pp. vii-viii.

books were actually published would have any effect on the holdings, it would presumably be in the direction of quality. There would be little motivation to acquire paperbound novels. There would be small motivation to buy novels at all, however, since English language and literature had no part in the curriculum. Later policy, with the advent of English departments, would have been on full collections of major authors. The University would be expected to have all titles (possibly all editions) of Cooper, Melville, and Hawthorne, but not of T. S. Arthur or Joseph H. Ingraham. The collection is very broad, however; of the 1,421 titles listed in Wright from 1830 to 1850, the University holds 728; of the 1,278 items in Wright 1851 to 1860, the University has 378.

This means that the University of Pennsylvania library has copies of 1,106 out of a possible 2,699 titles in the period, or about 40 per cent. The possibility of serious bias in a body of books approaching half of the total is very small. There is a higher number of books held by the library in the earlier part of the period, however, which weights the material in that direction.

The selection of the final sample from the University holdings was done by the following system. Copies of both volumes of Wright were marked in accordance with copies

or of the social or economic traits of American emigrants.
In its beginnings, the character of the confidential
family servant also seems derivative from convention,
rather than observed from American experience. The servant does develop into other directions.

Other Irish characters may be reasonably divided
according to the setting in which they appear; rural and
urban. The expectations of character and behavior differ
markedly for city Irish and country Irish, and the implications of these differences for the American imagination
follow this division. Each type will be treated in
a chapter.

A final chapter will examine the relation between
the Catholic imagery of the period and the Irish character.
Catholicism has qualities also largely determined by the
setting. Novels laid in Southern Europe and in French
and Spanish colonies present the church in Gothic and
highly political terms. Novels set in England and the
United States seldom show these characteristics. The
Irish type of Catholicism is examined in these contexts;
the Irish character is seen to be absolved from connection
with politically dangerous Catholic images.

II. TWO TRADITIONAL TYPES:
SOLDIER AND SERVANT

The Irish soldier and the Irish servant deserve a
separate treatment for two reasons. These two types were
a large portion of the Irish convention on the British
stage, and offer a ready standard for conventional aspects
in American fiction; they also differ from the rest of
the Irish characters, whose qualities depend heavily on
setting, in that both are independent of place. Soldiers
are soldiers, whether in cities or out of them. They take
their own society to the frontier or abroad, and their
qualities and behavior remain about the same. Servants
also follow their masters, and their function does not
depend on geography.

Military Irish

Over twenty books present Irish characters in the
American or British army or navy. Most of these characters are enlisted personnel, rather than officers; the
British tradition tended toward more officers than other
ranks.[1] The most useful way to reveal threads of common

---

[1]J. O. Bartley, Teaque, Shenkin and Sawney (Cork:
Cork University Press, 1954), p. 168. He lists 24 plays
with officers, only 8 with other ranks.

26

interest in these characters is to examine them in the periods of history in which the novels are set.

Four books which are set in colonial times contain Irish military characters. Roderick the Rover, by M. M. Ballou, is a swashbuckling romance about privateers and pirates in the Caribbean. There are two Irish gunners on the hero's ship, excellent fighters, "knocking an enemy on the head while they breathe a prayer for his soul."[2]

In The Brigantine, a novel concerning the conflicts between English and Dutch over New Amsterdam, an Irishman plays a considerable part. Paulus Spleutcher is his name--probably an alias to confuse the Dutch, though how he could manage to fool anyone with his thick brogue is a question. He is portrayed as brave, ingenious, and comic, and among other things he rescues an Englishman from prison.[3] "The Yellow Domino" is a long joke about a troop of Irish dragoons in France, who can afford only one ticket to a masked ball. One by one they go in, have a dance, and come out to hand the costume on.[4]

---

[2]Maturin Murray Ballou, Roderick the Rover; or, The Spirit of the Wave (Boston: F. Gleason, 1849), p. 26.

[3]The Brigantine; or, Admiral Lowe. A Tale of the 17th Century (New York: Crowen and Decker, 1839), pp. 43,47.

[4]"The Yellow Domino," in Humorist Tales: Being a Selection of Interesting Tales (New York: Nafis and Cornish; St. Louis: Nafis, Cornish and Co., 1841), pp. 53-55.

The last of these Irish before the Revolution is the only officer of the group, Lieutenant Molyneux, a villain in W. G. Simms' The Cassique of Kiawah.[5] As an officer, presumably Anglo-Irish, he is not strongly nationalized, and is expected to live up to the general moral code of people of his class. He is therefore judged more harshly than are any of the enlisted men.

There is very little to these pre-Revolutionary Irish, and nothing to violate the general conventional traits.

The American Revolution was a popular subject for all types of fiction. There are seven books in the sample with references to Irish characters in the war. Six of them are in the army, one in the navy; four of the characters are in the British service.

A midshipman on an American vessel in the anonymous Paul Jones speaks with a brogue, and shares the other "peculiarities" of his nation, to the amusement of the others on board. He tells jokes and tales of home, complaining about British judges who sentence the poor to be transported.[6] Elsewhere an officer tells the story of

---

[5] William Gilmore Simms, The Cassique of Kiawah: A Colonial Romance (New York: Redfield, 1859), passim.

[6] Paul Jones: A Tale of the Sea (Philadelphia: A. J. Rockefellar, 1843), p. 34.

Tim O'Donnell, a fortune hunter serving in the British
army before the war, who was tricked into marrying his
intended victim's spinster aunt.[7] In The Polish Chiefs,
a collection of legends about Pulaski and Kosciuszko,
Pulaski is quoted as admiring Irish soldiers because of
their love for combat.[8] Nothing beyond conventional qualities is made of Irish in these two books; comedy, brogue,
fortune-hunting, and love of fighting are all standard
attributes.

It is notable that there is little hostility expressed
toward Irish serving in the British forces in the Revolu-
tion. Two Irish soldiers appear in Henry Buckingham's
Harry Burnham, one of them a guard who lets an American
spy enter New York--for a bribe.[9] Two of Simms' novels,
The Kinsmen and The Partisan, both about the fighting in
South Carolina, suggest that Irish (with Germans and
Scotch) formed a large part of the British force,[10] and

---

[7]Paul Jones, p. 49.

[8]The Polish Chiefs: An Historical Romance (New York:
J. K. Porter, 1832), p. 74.

[9]Henry A. Buckingham, Harry Burnham, The Young Continental (New York: Burgess and Garrett; Baltimore: Burgess,
Taylor and Co., 1851), pp. 39, 248.

[10]William Gilmore Simms, The Kinsmen; or, The Black
Riders of the Congaree (Philadelphia: Lea and Blanchard,
1841), I, 69. A description of fresh, handsome Irish
regiment in the same, II, 69. In Simms, The Partisan:
A Tale of the Revolution (New York: Harper and Bros.,
1835), II, 107, a negro cook is told that Irish soldiers
will eat him.

that the Irish were not strongly committed to the British cause. A British officer orders an American left hanging to remind his Irish of the penalty for desertion.[11]

Camden, by John McClung, another novel about the Revolution in the South, presents two Irish troopers at somewhat greater length. Sam Dusky, a Virginian captured by the British, fights Larry, who is winning until the Virginian gouges and kicks him into submission, in the best frontier style, to the amusement of the other Irishman, Jerry Sullivan.[12] When Jerry is captured by the Americans, Sam Dusky protects him; he says they can shoot the Tories, but "'This is a real Irishman, and you shan't hurt a hair on his head.'"[13]

All of the Revolutionary treatments of the Irish, on either side, could be called friendly; this attitude may be partly based on the elements stressed in the convention: that Irish are comic, healthy, strong, friendly themselves. It seems clear also that the assumption that Irish were lukewarm toward the British is based largely on the later events in Ireland, in 1798 and after, when rebellion broke into the open. American writers from 1830

---

[11]Simms, The Kinsmen, II, 65.

[12]John Alexander McClung, Camden: A Tale of the South (Philadelphia: Carey and Lea, 1830), I, 42ff.

[13]McClung, Camden, I, 147.

on wrote with hindsight on this matter, and seem to have put anachronistic political views into their Irish characters' mouths. Looking back, they assume that Irish would have sympathized with American aims, England's difficulty being Ireland's opportunity.

A clear example of this is Barney Pike, in Caleb Wright's Wyoming, who will be treated more fully as a manservant in the later section. He is the first in town to enlist for the Revolution, because, as he says, Ireland expects it. He raises an American flag to mark the occasion, and leads a band of yokels against a Tory's house.[14] Barney has borrowed from later Irish political rhetoric.

Fourteen books deal with Irish military characters from Federal times up to the contemporary period. Most of these characters are unimportant, and add nothing new to the image. The Irish soldier or sailor is given to drink, or to blundering. When occasion arises, they are courageous.[15] The narrator of N. P. Willis' Inklings of

---

[14]Caleb E. Wright, Wyoming: A Tale (New York: Harper and Bros., 1845), pp. 19-40.

[15]In Swell Life at Sea; or, Fun, Frigates, and Yachting (New York: Stringer and Townsend, 1854), an Irish private, drunk, enters the wrong bedroom, in Malta, p. 320. Emily Edson Briggs, Ellen Parry; or, Trials of the Heart (New York: D. Appleton and Co.; Philadelphia: Geo. S. Appleton, 1850), Captain and Mrs. Ferrymore are perfect specimens of Irish charm, p. 96. Mrs. Caroline M. Kirkland, Western Clearings (New York: Wiley and Putnam, 1845), a dashing, possibly unreliable British Captain Maguire, p. 185. Mrs. Anna L. Snelling, Kabaosa; or,

Adventure shares a vessel on the Great Lakes with a
British regiment on its way back to Lower Canada. Most
of the complications are marital. Private O'Shea has
abducted a Canadian girl; to his dismay, the Colonel
forces him to marry her. Mahoney has brought aboard a
pregnant Indian, whom he absolutely refuses to marry. The
Colonel is driven to distraction by these matters--
he cries out, "Good God! these Irishmen!"[16]

Before moving to the three books which actually place
Irish soldiers and sailors into a living American problem,
it is necessary to point out the shallow and unoriginal

The Warriors of the West. A Tale of the Last War (New
York: Printed... by D. Adee, 1842), Paddy is a veteran of
the Indian wars, p. 157.

Irish also appear briefly in James Fenimore Cooper,
Afloat and Ashore; or, The Adventures of Miles Wallingford
(Philadelphia: Published by the Author, 1844), III, 177,
and J. F. Cooper, Ned Myers; or, A Life Before the Mast
(Philadelphia: Lea and Blanchard, 1843), p.99. And in
Joseph Holt Ingraham, The South-West. By A Yankee (New
York: Harper and Brothers), 1835, I, 165.

A whole roster of Irish appear as British naval offi-
cers--Captain, two Lieutenants and a villain--mostly
drinkers--in Mrs. Mary Stanley Shindler, The Young Sailor.
A Narrative Founded on Fact (New York: Harper and Brothers,
1843).

George Lippard, Legends of Mexico (Philadelphia: T. B.
Peterson, 1847), mentions an Irish teamster as a hero in
the Mexican war, p. 68; and Daniel Mallory, Short Stories
and Reminiscences of the Last Fifty Years. By an Old
Traveller (New York: Daniel Mallory, R. P. Bixby and Co.;
Philadelphia: Carey and Hart; Boston: Jordan and Co., 1842)
tells of an old Irishman who served under Mad Anthony
Wayne (presumably in the West), now kept in his government
post by General Harrison though past the ability to do
the work, II, 105.

[16]Nathaniel Parker Willis, Inklings of Adventure (New
York: Saunders and Otley, 1836), p. 48.

quality of most of the characters thus far noticed. A
surprising number of them are in the British service,
which removes them presumably from direct observation and
encourages the persistence of literary attitudes. Specifically, the trait of chasing women is frequent in this
group of books; this is a standard feature of the British
stage Irishman, but appears nowhere else in the American
version of the Irish. The conventionalism shown in these
military figures implies that the Irish soldier did not
attract enough interest to call for observation or development. He remains more a stock figure in anecdotes than
a character for constructive parts in fiction.

Justin Jones' Mad Jack and Gentleman Jack is basi-
cally an adventure story, set aboard the U.S.S. Constitu-
tion, but it raises the problem of Irish loyalty. There
is a conventionally comic Irish Marine, Teddy, who gets
drunk and lets his prisoner escape.[17] More interesting,
however, is the expressed feeling of Mad Jack, the captain
of Old Ironsides. On the first day of the cruise, he
orders nine sailors flogged:

> "I know these fellows well--they are Irishmen
> to a man, and I hate Irishmen. I wish the serv-
> ice was fairly rid of them."[18]

---

[17]Justin Jones, Mad Jack and Gentleman Jack; or, The
Last Cruise of Old Ironsides Around the World (Boston:
The Star Spangled Banner Office, 1850), pp. 59-60.

[18]Jones, Mad Jack, p. 35.

The hero, Gentleman Jack, deplores these sentiments, suggesting that Americans might enlist if they were not subject to flogging, and that Irish would work better if they were not abused.

Recollections of The United States Army manifests the same kind of division between conventional presentation of character and a social criticism. In the stories which comprise most of the book, Irish soldiers are treated in customary style. Though they are rough, violent, and quick to resent injuries, they are loyal and sympathetic generally. The autocratic tyranny of officers is a recurrent theme in the narratives. In one story, the soldiers plot to murder an officer. They ask an Irishman to join the conspiracy; he refuses, and tries to talk them out of it. After the crime is done, however, he refuses to turn his fellows in, and helps divert pursuit.[19] Another Irish soldier, driven beyond endurance by the persecution of a vicious officer, kills him; he then accepts his death sentence cheerfully, satisfied that he has done what he had to do.[20]

The preface to Recollections, however, raises the

---

[19]"Corporal Tim," in Recollections of The United States Army. A Series Of Thrilling Tales and Sketches. By an American Soldier (Boston: James Munroe and Co., 1845), pp. 4-6.

[20]"Fate of a Military Tyrant," Recollections of U.S. Army, p. 158.

question of the Irish from a totally different point of
view; namely, that the United States Army is composed
largely of foreigners. Two-thirds of the rank and file
are aliens; Irish, Scottish, Welsh, Danes, Swedes and so
on. As a consequence, there is no patriotism in the
ranks.[21] A similar point is made in Judson's The
Volunteer, which mentions a regiment of American deserters
in Santa Anna's army, made up of Irish, French and Germans
who joined their fellow Catholics on the Mexican side.[22]

In these three books the Irishman in military service
achieves at least one small facet of reality, of relation
to the American world, although the characters still
appear and behave according to conventional expectations.
The beginnings of a newer and altered image are present,
an image less determined by the British usage; but it is
safe to say that the Irish soldier as a type remained
largely unchanged. American authors did not use the character in important roles. The American context did not
significantly alter the British stereotype.

Servants

Irish servants display a wider range of function and
adaptation to American roles than the military do.

---

[21]Recollections of U.S. Army, p. viii.

[22]Edward Zane Carroll Judson, The Volunteer; or, The
Maid of Monterrey. By Ned Buntline (Boston: F. Gleason,
The Flag of our Union Office, 1847), p. 57.

Apparently the pressure of continual observation, because of the presence of immigrants as servants, brings a new image, more direct and lively than the stereotype of the military.

The character of the Irish servant began in a major way in American writing with Teague O'Regan, in Hugh Henry Brackenridge's _Modern Chivalry_. This book antedates the period of this study by some twenty years, but Teague is useful as a complete example of the original British conception of the Irish character. He will be examined in that light, and as the model for later American characters. Teague is used by Brackenridge as a vehicle for satirical commentary on the tendencies of American democracy, and therefore represents the failings of Americans, not those of the Irish only. For the purposes of this study, however, his character is examined only as an example of the Irish type at the beginning of its American career.

Teague is clearly derivative from the British tradition, and Brackenridge's account of the choice of the Irishman acknowledges the debt:

> It has been asked, why, in writing this memoir;
> have I taken my clown, _from the Irish nation_?
> The character of the English clown, I did not well
> understand; nor could I imitate the manner of
> speaking. . . . The American has in fact, yet,
> no character; neither the clown, nor the gentle-
> man. So that I could not take one from our own
> country; which I would much rather have done,

as the scene lay here. But the midland states
of America, and the western parts in general,
being half Ireland, the character of the Irish
clown, will not be wholly misunderstood. It
is true the clown is taken from the aboriginal
Irish; a character not so well known in the
North of that country; nevertheless, it is still
so much known, even there, and amongst the emigrants here, or their descendants, that it will
not be wholly thrown away.

On the Irish stage, it is a standing character; and on the theatre in Britain, it is
also introduced.[23]

It is interesting that Brackenridge should choose an

"aboriginal," rather than an Ulsterman, almost entirely

on the ground that the character was ready made. His

"bog-trotter" is illiterate; like most "aboriginal Irish"

he has "a great assurance of countenance, but little

information, or literature."[24]

Teague also has "a too great fondness for women,"[25]

a weakness which he manifests by jumping into bed with

a maidservant early in his adventures. His self-assurance

is called on here, and he succeeds in shifting the blame

to an innocent clergyman.[26] Teague is not handsome, how-

ever, nor does he enjoy fighting; he is terrified when

Captain Farrago urges him to fight a duel.[27] His chief

---

[23]Hugh Henry Brackenridge, Modern Chivalry, ed. Claude
M. Newlin (New York: American Book Co., 1937), p. 405.
First published 1792-1815.

[24]Brackenridge, Modern Chivalry, p. 15.

[25]Brackenridge, Modern Chivalry, p. 15.

[26]Brackenridge, Modern Chivalry, p. 30.

[27]Brackenridge, Modern Chivalry, pp. 49-51.

traits so far as the plot of the book is concerned are
his absolute faith in his competence for any position--
in Congress, in the American Philosophical Society, or on
the judicial bench--and his utter lack of proper humility.
He is used by Brackenridge to comment on the democratic
system: "If I were to go into any deliberative body, and
pull out the first man that occurred to me, nine times
out of ten I would find I had a Teague O'Regan by the
tail."[28]   It is perhaps prophetic that the Irishman should
be used to symbolize the strain on government later aggra-
vated by the immigrant urban masses.

Teague is then a character almost completely
described by the British stage convention; the conservatism of the image is shown by his name, and by the epithet
"bog-trotter," both characteristic of 17th century Irish
figures.   Amorousness, brashness, and blarney are also
regular conventional traits.   He differs only in his ugliness and cowardice, both traits demanded by his comic
position.

We will first examine a group of Irish servants of
the same general type as Teague, that is, personal servants.   They all have fairly large parts to play in their
books; none is a very close copy of Teague, partly because
none fills precisely the same function of criticizing

---

[28]Brackenridge, Modern Chivalry, p. 674.

the democratic ideal. The degree of variation from
the conventional type defined by Teague, however, gives
an insight into the persistence of some qualities and
into the emergence of a new Irish image.

As already suggested, the two succeeding sections of
this paper examine Irish characters in urban and rural
sections, to demonstrate the differences in possible roles
and to determine the significance of the differences.
The relation of a servant to his master varies according
to the kind of service involved; but especially with the
personal servants discussed here, geography is practically
incidental. The servant may be required to travel with
the master, after the pattern of Teague or Sancho Panza.
In the books discussed here, the servants find their way
into the army and the navy, and go to Texas and Canada,
Virginia and New Orleans, in the course of following the
fortunes of the people and the families they serve. The
important thing is not where they are, but the type of
close dependence on the master that they show. The kind
of plot which faces them, and the kind of problems--
slavery, crime, war--do help distinguish these characters
from each other.

Two of these personal servants, quite similar to
each other, resemble Teague more than the others. Barney
Pike, of Wright's Wyoming, mentioned above, is almost

a caricature of the Irish body-servant. He appears as
a family retainer in the Susquehanna valley of Pennsylvania. He "spent every last penny to get to America"
from County Antrim,[29] arriving with a thick brogue,
a ready tongue, and a rosary in his trunk. The American
maid, Peggy, finds the rosary, and her apprehensions about
Catholic witchcraft lead to a comic exchange with
Barney.[30]

When the Revolution breaks out, Barney is eager to
go, as noted above. He and his master, Walter Henderson,
arrive in Canada. Barney serves as a guard in an American
prison. The complicated plot includes a mysterious
priest, ultimately revealed to be the heroine's father,
who uses his office to sway Barney. All the tangles are
resolved by the American victory, a happy return to
Pennsylvania, and Barney's marriage to Peggy.

Barney resembles Teague most in the nature of the
bond between himself and the family he serves. He has no
life apart from them; he is expected to go with the master, where possible; when he marries, it is the maid. He
knows his place, and settles into it for life. He is
given a fair share of the attention, and some good lines,
but he is no more than comic relief. At the same time,

[29]Wright, Wyoming, p. 19.

[30]Wright, Wyoming, pp. 15-17.

he differs from Teague in the anachronistic realism
given to his political views and to the process of emigration. He is less traditional, more in touch with the
situation of mid-century in this; and he is not used to
point the dangers of democracy, as Teague was.

The loyal retainer in Orlando Melville is also
Barney, no surname given. Like Barney Pike, he is
"jovial, happy, careless," and would gladly die for his
master. As the narrator says, "instances of such devotion
are not uncommon among the lower orders of the Irish population."[31] Barney is balanced in this novel--which is
actually set in England--by Sambo, the heroine's equally
devoted Negro servant.

Barney and Orlando Melville fall victims to a press
gang; behind this is an evil British lieutenant who lusts
after the heroine, Kate Loraine. Aboard ship, the other
prisoners falsely accuse Barney of theft; but he defends
himself so well, and is so loyal, that the captain makes
him a steward. Eventually all are freed by Decatur in
the U.S.S. United States, reunited with Kate and Sambo,
and return to England.

Barney throughout is a paragon of strength and en-
couragement for his master, loyal and upright and clever,

[31]E. Curtiss Hine, Orlando Melville; or, The Victims
of the Pressgang (Boston: F. Gleason, cop. 1848), p. 13.

though comic in speech and brash in behavior. Like
Barney Pike, he is comic relief, and a companion in
adventure; like him also, he is content to keep his servant's place, though he has shown considerable competence
in a crisis. Both demonstrate the good humor, loyalty,
and docility of the Irish type. They resemble Teague in
their free manners, colorful language, and servant's role;
they differ in being brave, respecting women, and staying
in their places.

Both of these Barneys also show how strong a factor
patriotic sentiment can be; the adventures are black and
white, British and American, and little complexity can
enter (though there are endless complications). The simplicity of the conception of the Irish character, and the
laziness of its execution, are related to this generally
slack and conventional approach to the novels.

John Beauchamp Jones' Wild Western Scenes is at least
free from patriotic distortions. It is a book of Southwestern adventure, often humorous, without a strong central plot. Joe Beck is the devoted Irish servant of
Mr. Glenn, a Philadelphian, travelling in Texas. Joe is
the victim of the practical jokes which the Texans might
otherwise have played on his master. He is comic in a
passive way, chiefly in his pathetic reactions to apparent
danger. His tormentor, Sneak, loads Joe's gun with a

double charge, which knocks him down. Later he puts

asafoetida in Joe's moccasins, attracting wolves which

chase Joe up a tree. Pecked by a hen, Joe thinks he is

dying of snake-bite; refusing a Bible and an Episcopal

prayer book, he demands a priest and "the ointment."[32]

The comic deathbed scene comes back; this time Joe prays

the Lord's Prayer in Latin, terrifying Sneak.[33]

Joe Beck has no brogue, but is blunderingly loyal

to his nation:

> St. Patrick forbid that I should be anything
> but an Irishman! I should like to know if an
> Irishman ain't as good as anybody else, particu-
> larly when he's born in America, as I was?[34]

This weak bull is another note in Joe Beck's comic

character. He is less outrageously a caricature than the

two Barneys, because his motivation is in a lower key.

He remains a stock character, however, stiff and unreal,

because his naivete, cowardice, and bluster are assumed

to fill out his comic role. Like the other characters,

Joe Beck accepts his servant's role, and is defined by it.

He cannot be imagined apart from his master.

The Irish coachman turned manservant, Jimmy O'Brien,

---

[32]John Beauchamp Jones, Wild Western Scenes: A Narrative of Adventures in the Western Wilderness, Forty Years
Ago (Philadelphia: E. Ferrett and Co., 1845), p. 244.

[33]J. B. Jones, Wild Western Scenes, p. 99.

[34]J. B. Jones, Wild Western Scenes, p. 214.

in the pseudonymous Mr. Frank, The Underground Mail-Agent,
marks a change in this group, at least in his mobility
and relative independence. He is first encountered in
a Philadelphia crowd listening to Fitznoosle, an English
anti-slavery agitator. Jimmy reveals that Fitznoosle is
the absentee landlord of his home village, and describes
at length the brutal treatment given to the Irish.[35] For
this outburst, Jimmy is fired. Taken on as a personal
servant by Mr. Frank, Jimmy is overjoyed; but as to
Mr. Frank's project of freeing Negroes in the South,
he says:

> "I think more good could be done by attemptin'
> somethin' for the oppressed, beggared, ʌn' praste-
> ridden poor ov ould Ireland—for, sure, they
> stand more in nade of it!"[36]

Jimmy is belligerent in his defense of the poor.
When a policeman tries to arrest a beggar-woman, he
assaults him physically and verbally to rescue her.[37]
That the woman's daughter, who had just died, had been
an unemployed mantua-maker points again to the author's
uses for Jimmy O'Brien. He is meant to draw attention
to the oppression of the poor of the North, in a context
which makes the slavery of the Negro seem mild. Jimmy

---

[35]Vidi, Mr. Frank, The Underground Mail-Agent (Philadelphia: Lippincott, Grambo, and Co., 1853), pp. 76-79.

[36]Vidi, Mr. Frank, p. 115.

[37]Vidi, Mr. Frank, p. 118.

refers to the desperate condition of Ireland, which is
hardly ever mentioned anywhere else; he complains of his
treatment when leaving his employer, "Hard curses, bad
aiting, and worse payin', ain't timptation for ony man
to remain."[38] Though Jimmy is still, in conventional
style, emotional, demonstrative, and comic in person,
the dimension added to his character by his social comments on inequality and empty philanthropy makes him seem
a more realistic character--that is, one more in touch
with a complex world.

Another Irish servant, from 1830, presents a different social problem. In Catherine Maria Sedgwick's
Clarence, Conolly, a fresh immigrant, serves as a male
nurse to a rich invalid. The New York streets in the
novel have plenty of Irish, selling oranges, gathering in
muttering groups on corners. One such "knot of Irishmen,"
with their "combustible passions," threatens a doctor who
has let an Irishman die without calling a priest.[39] The
same doctor is involved in the deathbed will of Conolly's
employer. Angered at the doctor, and needing money to
help his family to emigrate, Conolly takes a bribe for
false testimony. He is the center of interest in the

---

[38]Vidi, Mr. Frank, p. 75.

[39]Catherine Maria Sedgwick, Clarence; or, A Tale of
Our Times (Philadelphia: Carey and Lea, 1830), I, 74.

courtroom episodes, evoking commentary on the problems of assimilation. Attacking his credibility, an attorney describes him as

> "an ignorant, unprincipled foreigner, who had no name and no stake in society. . . . There were thousands of such men in the city, they could be picked up anywhere, from the swarms about the Cathedral, to the dens of Catherine-lane, . . ."[40]

a description which emphasizes the instability and root-lessness of the immigrants, and the danger they offer to American institutions.

It is also said of Conolly that he is "a compound of good-heartedness and the absence of all principle, and all that mixture of simplicity and cunning that characterizes his excitable and imaginative nation";[41] which is both an excellent definition of a child, and a kind of excuse for his actions. His simplicity provides humor; in trying to give his name to the court, he must explain the whole family system of peasant Ireland. In various contexts he would identify himself as McCormic, Conolly, and Ford.[42] This again helps to show how simple he is. His main motives in his perjury are loyalty to his religion and to his family; however mistaken these motives are, they are at least human and intelligible. And his final act in

---

[40]Sedgwick, Clarence, I, 96.

[41]Sedgwick, Clarence, I, 90.

[42]Sedgwick, Clarence, I, 89-90.

the novel is to tell the truth, save the hero's case, and disappear into prison.

Conolly has a substantial role, and the springs of his action are well defined in his personal sphere. He seems therefore impressively round as a character, compared to the others so far noted, in spite of his being made childish. The strong emphasis on family and Ireland is remarkable. Among those characters who refer to Ireland, Conolly is notable for the lack of special pleading. Jimmy O'Brien uses Ireland to deflate an Abolitionist, others will use it to arouse sympathy for immigrants, but Conolly simply acknowledges his relatives. The religious motive also seems natural and unstrained. Without anti-Catholic tone, the demand for confession before death is reasonable, and the doctor's indifference seems understandable.

If Conolly and Jimmy O'Brien have moved away from the old concept of the family retainer toward being employees, with lives of their own, they have gained in flexibility and realism. The relationship established between servant and mistress in the anonymous Estelle Grant is a mutual dependence, almost a friendship. All hint of financial superiority in the mistress is gone; only the barriers of class remain.

The book relates the destruction of the heroine's

life by her villainous husband, and her consequent sufferings and revenge. The crime and violence of this
story, and its scenes of low life, provide another new
context for the Irish servant.

Kate O'Donnell's family was put out of its home by
Mr. Emory; Effie Johnson, whom she liked very much, was
seduced and abandoned by him; Kate looks after a sick man
whom Emory ruined in business. When Mr. Grant falls prey
to Emory, therefore, Kate tries to help the family. She
warns Estelle Grant about him, but she is forced to marry
him by her father's failure.

Kate carries a letter to Estelle from one of Emory's
women; Estelle thereupon leaves him. From this moment on,
Kate is her constant companion, confidante, and helper.
They live for a time in a "crib," a slum tenement in
New York; later they travel through the South together.
In New Orleans, Kate fights in the street with blacks when
they call her an "Irish thief." Estelle tells her not to
fight; "not that I have any sympathy for the negroes, who
might be cut piecemeal for all I should care." Kate sub-
sides: "Iv ye knew how I hate the nagurs!"[43] Through
their degradation they remain very close, much more equal
than any of the other pairs. Together they plan two mur-
ders, one of them successful. When Estelle dies, Kate

_____

[43]Estelle Grant; or, The Lost Wife (New York: Garrett
and Co., cop. 1855), pp. 208-209.

drowns herself in the East River. This act alone would
set her apart from the other servants; it is striking,
decisive, and central to the action, not a customary or
polite ending like Barney Pike's marriage. Kate plays
a major part, virtually equal in interest to that of the
heroine. Though they are formally mistress and maid,
Kate is better equipped than Estelle for survival in the
slums.

The Housewife's Burden: The Irish Girl

In the conventional portrayal of the relation between
master and servant, fixed devotion, deep and lasting, is
assumed on both sides. The servant wants nothing more
than to serve for life, and to have his children serve
the master's children. The reality, for the merchants'
and clerks' wives who employed Irish girls during the
period, may have been difficult. Hiring, keeping, and
handling domestic help tactfully is a problem that crops
up in several books.

Most of T. S. Arthur's work consists of instructive
tales, designed to inculcate sound business habits and
careful domestic economy. Wisdom and self-control in
dealing with servants are the concern of two of his stories in the sample. Mrs. Eldridge, for example, having
herself caused chaos in the kitchen, takes it out on the
cook: "Leave my sight and the house this instant, you

miserable Irish trollop!" To which the poor cook mildly assents.[44]

In the second tale, an irascible housewife hires Irish Nancy as cook. Harassed by constant criticism, Nancy burns the dinner and quits immediately.[45] The moral in both stories is that the young housewife must learn to control herself before she can make a happy, comfortable, efficient home for her husband. Inexperience in managing a household with servants, possibly because the mistress is reaching higher in the social order, is the great difficulty.

The same point is made in W. T. Adams's "Good for Nothings." Two employers are described. Mrs. Bagley treats her Bridget kindly, and gives her every third Sunday off. She recognizes that "these Irish girls are human beings . . . and need a little recreation."[46] Her friend, Mrs. Veazie, has no conception of proper treatment of her Margaret. She tries to force the girl to shovel a pile of coal into the cellar. Margaret refuses, on

---

[44]Timothy Shay Arthur, What Can Woman Do? (Boston: L. P. Crown; Philadelphia: J. W. Bradley, 1855), p. 67.

[45]T. S. Arthur, "A Peevish Day, and its Consequences," The Home Mission (Boston: L. P. Crown and Co.; Philadelphia: J. W. Bradley, 1853), p. 147.

[46]William Taylor Adams, In Doors and Out; or, Views from the Chimney Corner. By Oliver Optic (Boston: Brown, Bazin and Co., 1855), p. 25.

the reasonable ground that it is a job for a man.

Mrs. Veazie can't see why:

> "These girls are used to working in the fields
> in Ireland, digging turf and pounding stones.
> I don't see why they should be so stuck up when
> they come to America."[47]

She dismisses Margaret for insubordination. Mrs. Bagley
takes the girl into her house, and under proper treatment
she develops into a very good worker.

Snobbery and pretension are the vices of the employers; servants who express themselves are thought bold by
the excessively refined. Jane, a "short, stout, sandy-
haired, freckle-faced daughter of the 'Ould Sod,'" offends
Miss Tenniswood, a visitor, by her manner. Miss Tenniswood comments on the deplorable trend toward "independence
and equality" among servants.[48] The heroine rebukes her
for her aristocratic prejudice.

The Loveleisures, the aptly named couple in _Means_
Without _Living_, are criticized for following a crackpot
theory instead of keeping their household running. They
have stopped cooking, and have laid off their maid Jane,
who is left with a sick mother and no income. When
Mrs. Loveleisure meets Jane in the street, and asks sym-
pathetically about her mother, Jane replies bitterly that

---

[47]Adams, _In_ _Doors_, p. 27.

[48]Oran, _The_ _Outcast_; _or_, _A_ _Season_ _in_ _New_ _York_
(New York: Peabody and Co., 1833), p. 37.

"'the bit wages to comfort the mother 'ud a been better than a daughter at home, to help ate what wasn't to be had.'"[49] The foolish act of the Loveleisures in cutting down expenses when they have plenty of money, affects the whole economy. The rich, the book suggests, are morally obliged to carry out their role as consumers and employers.

Another touchy problem is the care of Catholic servants in Protestant households. Polly, an Irish girl in Sara Josepha Hale's "Boarding Out," sets as conditions of a job that she must have "the privilege of going to the Church of the Holy Cross on Sundays, and keeping Lent."[50] This is a neat and realistic detail; Lenten regulations might complicate life for the employer, requiring separate meals on Wednesdays and Fridays, and possibly a lightened work load because of fasting.

For a zealous Protestant employer, the challenge of the Catholic maid is a supreme test of tact, self-control, and psychology. Louisa Tuthill, in The Belle, The Blue, and The Bigot, presents, in the regular allegorical fashion, two contrasting women. Gabriella Duncan, the "bigot," is a religious enthusiast who lets her zeal distort her

---

[49]Means Without Living (Boston: Weeks, Jordan and Co., 1837), p. 58.

[50]Sara Josepha Hale, "Boarding Out." A Tale of Domestic Life (New York: Harper and Brothers, 1846), p. 63.

perspectives. "I told [Biddy] yesterday that she believed in a pack of absurdities."[51] She tells her friend
Joanna how to handle her maid:

"If you do not intend to remove that bigoted
Roman Catholic Catharine from the nursery, you
will tell her very plainly . . . that you think
her perfectly heathenish in her idolatry."[52]

The nursery, of course, would be an especially sensitive
position for possible effects on future generations.
Joanna agrees that "Romish servants" are a trial to good
employers, but she prefers to use more indirect methods.

Their methods are put to the test. The priest questions both Biddy and Catharine about their employers.
Biddy easily recognizes the hostility in Gabriella, but
Catharine defends Joanna against the priest. Angry at
this, he orders her to leave her position, but a child is
sick and she stays, because of loyalty and affection for
Joanna. As a result, she is afraid to meet the priest,
stays away from church, and finally becomes an Episcopalian. Biddy remains a truculent and defensive Catholic.
So, tact, kindness, and subtlety produce the desired
result, while overbearing authority fails.

It is clear that in this group of Irish maids--

---

[51]Louisa Caroline Tuthill, The Belle, The Blue and
The Bigot; or, Three Fields for Woman's Influence (Providence: Samuel C. Blodget, 1844), p. 257.

[52]Tuthill, The Belle, p. 256.

servants as social problems--all of the traditional Irish
marks are gone. They are not comic, not blundering, not
dashing or amorous. They are drawn apparently very close
to life; this was one area, it seems, where sharp observation came into play. Their roles are not large, and they
are of interest only as a problem in domestic harmony,
important enough for a moral tale, but not an imaginative
plot.

Minor Servants

The broad popularity of the Irish servant, examined
in a dozen books already, is shown by the presence of such
characters in twenty-eight more books. Few of the thirty-
six servants make more than a very brief appearance. The
qualities of these servants tend to be mildly conventional
again, possibly because they are minor and need a note to
make them interesting. They are noisy, careless, and
untidy on the one hand, and good-hearted, faithful, and
shrewd on the other. All but five of the servants are
women; the Irish maid is the general rule. This is the
same as the pattern in the previous section, in which all
nine of the characters are women; but the reverse of the
group of major, traditional servants, five out of six of
whom were men.

About half the women are called Biddy or Bridget.
Sixteen of the group have a brogue; most of the others

have no lines. Blunders in speech are strong in only
one character,[53] and there is only one weak bull.[54] None
of these servants have any family, and their relation with
their employers is not strongly defined.[55]

---

[53]Harry Spofford, The Mysteries of Worcester; or,
Charley Temple and His First Glass of Liquor (Worcester:
Published by H. J. Capp, 1846), p. 28.

[54]Harriot F. Curtis, Jessie's Flirtations (New York:
Harper and Brothers, 1846), p. 87: "I'll not be saying
anything about the kay's being found until it's lost."

[55]The twenty-six other books in which Irish servants
appear:
Mrs. J. T. Bickford, Scandal (Boston: Shepard, Clark and
Brown, 1857), maid, I, 297; another, I, 334.
Robert Montgomery Bird, Sheppard Lee (New York: Harper
and Brothers, 1836), maid, I, 143.
Osgood Bradbury, Ellen Grant; or, Fashionable Life in New
York (New York: Dick and Fitzgerald, Printers, n.d.),
maid, 69.
Sarah Elizabeth Bradford, Lewie; or, The Bended Twig
(Auburn: Alden, Beardsley, and Co.; Rochester: Wanzer,
Beardsley and Co., 1853), cook, I, 28.
David Brown, The Planter; or, Thirteen Years in the South
(Philadelphia: H. Hooker, 1853), maid, p. 9.
John Delavan Bryant, Pauline Seward: A Tale of Real Life
(Baltimore: John Murphy; Pittsburg: George Quigley;
Dublin: R. Grace and Sons, 1847), cook, I, 205.
Oliver Bell Bunce, Life Before Him (New York: W. A.
Townsend and Co., 1860), maid, p. 264.
Confessions of a Female Inebriate; or, Intemperance in
High Life (Boston: William Henshaw, 1842), maid, p. 20.
Edward H. Dixon, M.D., Scenes in the Practice of a New
York Surgeon (New York: Robert M. DeWitt, cop. 1855),
maids referred to, p. 29.
Mary Jane Holmes, Dora Deane; or, The East India Uncle.
And Maggie Miller; or, Old Hagar's Secret (New York:
C. M. Saxton, 1859). Two novels bound together; two women
in Dora Deane, pp. 20, 182; girl in Maggie Miller, p. 273.
Jane Elizabeth Hornblower, Vara; or, The Child of Adoption
(New York: Robert Carter and Brothers, 1854), girl, p. 236.
Martha Hubbell, The Shady Side; or, Life in a Country
Parsonage (Boston: John P. Jewett; Cleveland: Jewett,

Perhaps the prominence of the Irish servant in the
American mind is best exemplified in two remarks on their
absence. A Yankee woman in Illinois regrets that there
are no Irish or negro maids to be found;[56] and Cooper,

Proctor, and Worthington; London: Low and Co., 1853),
girl, pp. 291-292.
Joseph Holt Ingraham, Jemmy Daily; or, The Little News
Vender (Boston: Brainard and Co., 1843), maid, p. 37;
porter, p. 35.
Isabel; or, The Trials of the Heart (New York: Harper and
Brothers, 1845), maid, p. 50.
Emily Judson, Trippings in Author-Land. By Fanny Forester
(New York: Paine and Burgess, 1846), nurse, p. 19.
Knickerbocker Gallery, maid, in J. M. Legare, "The Loves
of Mary Jones." Mallory, Short Stories, maid, p. 36.
Sara Payson Parton, Fresh Leaves. By Fanny Fern (New York:
Mason Brothers, 1857), maid and manservant, p. 164; boot-
black, p. 221; maid, p. 221.
Elizabeth Phelps, The Tell-Tale; or, Home Secrets Told by
Old Travellers (Boston: Phillips, Sampson and Co., 1853),
maids, pp. 54, 120.
William Price, Clement Falconer; or, The Memoirs of a
Young Whig (Baltimore: N. Hickman, 1838), maid, p. 167.
Anna Cora Ritchie, The Fortune Hunter; or, The Adventures
of a Man About Town (New York: J. Winchester, New World
Press, cop. 1844), maid, p. 59.
Martha Russell, Leaves From the Tree Igdrasyl (Boston:
John P. Jewett; Cleveland: Jewett, Proctor, and Worthing-
ton; New York: Sheldon, Lamport, and Blakeman, 1854),
maid, p. 125.
Ben Shadow (pseud.), Echoes of a Belle; or, A Voice From
the Past (New York: George P. Putnam and Co., 1853),
maid, p. 160.
Ann Sophia Stephens, Fashion and Famine (New York: Bunce
and Brother, 1854), kitchen helper, p. 130.
George H. Throop, Lynde Weiss: An Autobiography (Philadelphia: Lippincott, Grambo and Co., 1852), maid, p. 58;
boy, p. 58; man, p. 147.

[56]Eliza Woodson Farnham, Life in Prairie Land (New
York: Harper and Brothers, 1846), p. 149.

with his frequent nostalgia for an earlier, less compli-

cated world, admires a servant who is

> neither an Irishman nor a black, but a regular,
> old-fashioned Manhattanese coachman; a class
> apart, and of whom, in the confusion of tongues
> that pervades the modern Babel, a few still
> remain, like monuments of the past, scattered
> along the Appian Way.[57]

Summary

On the basis of the sample, the Irish soldier does

not seem to occupy a vital or interesting place in the

American imagination. Such characters as do appear are

mainly in the context of war novels, in which stereotypes

of motive and character prevent effective or realistic

development of the type. In these stories, the most

interesting facet of the Irishman is his Americanism;

assumptions about Irish political feelings make the

authors see the Irish as siding with the United States

against Britain. Only in a few books does any hint of

a social complication appear, with questions on Irish

assimilation; but these questions do not arise in the

plots of stories.

Irish servants are more common in the fiction, and

show a far greater range of possible behavior. Many of

the servants with the largest roles are, it is true, cast

---

[57]James Fenimore Cooper, The Ways of the Hour
(New York: George P. Putnam, 1850), p. 89.

into the older, more traditional image of faithful
retainer, in complete economic and emotional dependence
on the master, after the fashion of Teague. They neither
want nor need a private life. So also those servants who
are least developed, who make momentary appearances, are
likely to be in a shallow Irish mold.

But two of the major servants, and the group of
problem servants, show a different image. They appear
as free agents economically, employees rather than feudal
dependents. They have rights, make demands, and seem more
like actual participants in the society. The traditional
devotion is gone; but so is the traditional generosity
and power of the master. As the style of master changes
to the harried middle-class merchant, trying to keep up
appearances, so does the image of the servant.

Except for the group of traditional servants, most of
the characters, as we have seen, are women; the imbalance
is rectified in the following chapter, on Irish in the
city. Most of the women are maids, most of the men are
laborers.

III. IRISH IN THE CITY

This section will deal with those Irish characters
who appear in plots or sections of books which take place
in cities. Most of these settings are Eastern, most often
New York. There are a good many books eligible under this
criterion: excluding servants in cities, who have been
treated already, there are over fifty books with material
of interest.

The Atmosphere of the City

The first encounter of a young American, in the city
for the first time, may be with an Irish apple-woman;[1] or
the green newcomer may think an Irish coachman has given
him a ride out of pure generosity.[2] Or an Irish beggar
may accost him.[3]

Irish families have crowded into tenements, turning
respectable neighborhoods into slums, to the humiliation

---

[1]Joseph Holt Ingraham, The Dancing Feather; or, The
Amateur Freebooters. A Romance of New York (Boston: George
Roberts, 1842), p. 23. The young man is arrested after
an altercation over payment.

[2]Ingraham, The Gipsy of The Highlands; or, The Jew
and The Heir (Boston: Redding and Co., 1843), p. 12.

[3]John Beauchamp Jones, The Life and Adventures of a
Country Merchant (Philadelphia: Lippincott, Grambo, and
Co., 1854), p. 260.

of native Americans too poor to move away.[4] They are
the non-paying and ungrateful patients of young doctors
building a practice, and of old doctors who have lost
theirs, possibly through drink.[5] Charitable Americans
call on Irish families when they need help;[6] friendly
Irish help others when they can.[7] Poor Irish children
are taken into Protestant Sunday schools.[8]

---

[4]Which, The Right, Or The Left? (New York: Garrett
and Co., 1855), a nice Protestant laundress lives among
Irish, p. 129; William Leete Stone, Ups and Downs in the
Life of a Distressed Gentleman (New York: Leavitt, Lord
and Co.; Boston: Crocker and Brewster, 1836), in which
the hero lives in a hovel, with "several" Irish families
in the two upstairs rooms, p. 171.

[5]Edward H. Dixon, M.D., Scenes in the Practice of
a New York Surgeon (New York: Robert DeWitt, cop. 1855)
is particularly bitter about the instability and unrelia-
bility of the poor Irish, p. 260. Elizabeth Phelps,
"First Trials of a Young Physician," The Tell-Tale; or,
Home Secrets Told by Old Travellers (Boston: Phelps,
Sampson and Co., 1853), pp. 246-248, two of the doctor's
first patients are Irish. The father of the hero in
Ingraham, Jemmy Daily; or, The Little News Vender
(Boston: Brainard and Co., 1843) is a doctor reduced by
drink to treating Irish in the Boston slums, p. 12.

[6]Oran, The Outcast; or, A Season in New York (New
York: Peabody and Co., 1833), I, 104; the principal characters visit a bereaved Irish family. In Isabel; or,
Trials of the Heart (New York: Harper and Bros., 1845),
p. 127, the heroine helps Irish children whose father has
nearly drowned. Martha Russell, Leaves From the Tree
Igdrasyl (Boston: John P. Jewett; Cleveland: Proctor and
Worthington; New York: Sheldon, Lamport and Blakeman,
1854), p. 39, a doctor sends Christmas dinner to an Irish
family.

[7]Russell, Leaves From The Tree, p. 70ff; an Irish
flower-seller, with a German immigrant, cares for a crippled American child until her family takes her.

[8]Isabel, p. 127; Sara Payson Parton, Fresh Leaves.
By Fanny Fern (New York: Mason Brothers, 1857), p. 327.

Irish are everywhere in the streets, driving coaches
or drays, pushing wheelbarrows, carrying hods, or peddling
flowers or apples.[9] They heckle street preachers, play
the accordion in street cars, laugh and drink atop a
cab.[10]

The Irish add a note of truculence to life in the
city. "'Get out of the way, you old Paddy,'" says an
American to an Irishwoman. "'And indade I won't . . .
I'll get right _in_ your way,'" comes the response.[11] An
Irish boatman in New York calls Ned Myers a "Yankee son
of a _____," and takes Myers to court when he retaliates.[12]

---

[9]Coachmen: Silas P. Holbrook, Sketches, by a Travel-
ler (Boston: Carter and Hendee, 1830), p. 88; T. S. Arthur,
Sketches of Life and Character (Philadelphia: J. W. Brad-
ley, 1850), p. 170; Ingraham, Gipsy of the Highlands,
p. 12; Lloyd Wharton Bickley, The Aristocrat: An American
Tale (Philadelphia: Key and Biddle, 1833), II, 158.
Wheelbarrow, Asa Greene, The Perils of Pearl Street,
Including a Taste of the Dangers of Wall Street (New York:
Betts and Anstice, and Peter Hill, 1834), p. 127. Hod
Carriers: Cornelius Capricorn, Speculations on the Comet
(New York: James Kelly, 1832), Ch. III. Cf. references to
hods in Ann Sophia Stephens, High Life in New York. By
Jonathan Slick, Esq. (New York, 1843), p. 10. Apple
Seller, Ingraham, Dancing Feather, p. 23.

[10]Street preacher incident in Mortimer Neal Thomson,
Doesticks' Letters: And What He Says (Philadelphia: T. B.
Peterson and Bros., cop. 1855), p. 109. Accordion, Parton,
Fresh Leaves, p. 264. Loafers, Ingraham, The American
Lounger; or, Tales, Sketches and Legends (Philadelphia:
Lea and Blanchard, 1839), p. 40.

[11]Lydia Maria Child, Letters From New York. Second
Series (New York: C. S. Francis and Co., 1845), p. 167.

[12]James Fenimore Cooper, ed., Ned Myers; or, A Life
Before the Mast (Philadelphia: Lea and Blanchard, 1843),
p. 18.

In fact, Irish characters seem thoroughly at home in
court; they enjoy their parts, whether as plaintiffs,
witnesses, or defendants. It seems that most scenes laid
in courts or police stations show an Irishman involved
in some scrape. The hero of William Leete Stone's Ups and
Downs in the Life of a Distressed Gentleman is tried for
assaulting a neighbor, an Irishwoman, for example.[13] The
Irish are not intimidated by the law, and are quick to
call on the courts in defense of their rights.

Aggressive, poor, noisy, violent, the Irish are a
large element in the texture of life in the American city
of the period. These qualities may be disturbing, but
may also add excitement and color to the city. Mortimer
Neal Thomson, in his humorous Doesticks' Letters, gives
a racy account of New York seen by his narrator, just come
to New York. Doesticks describes the streets, the thea-
ters, and the diversions of the city; and he meets Irish
everywhere. His landlady is a one-eyed Irishwoman, and
his bed is full of bugs.[14] A guard encountered on the
Battery is "a dilapidated Hibernian,"[15] and a man involved

---

[13]Stone, Ups and Downs, p. 216; there are two such
incidents with Irish in Oran, The Outcast, pp. 8, 56; and
a long trial in Catherine Maria Sedgwick, Clarence; or,
A Tale of Our Times (Philadelphia: Carey and Lea, 1830),
I, 87.

[14]Thomson, Doesticks' Letters, p. 51.

[15]Thomson, Doesticks' Letters, p. 42.

in a theater brawl is taken away by "the Emerald conserva-
tors of the public quiet."[16] According to a fortune tel-
ler, a "squint-eyed Irishman" stole Doesticks' knife, and
he loses his coat to an Irishman in a fight between fire
companies, because he "ain't big enough to lick him."[17]

The streets of New York are full of dirty immigrants,
German and Irish;[18] Doesticks' militia company, "The
Lager-Bier American Volunteers and Native Empire City
Shillelagh Guards," is composed of "Irish, Dutch, Span-
iards, and Sandwich Islanders--the only Americans in the
company being the colored target-bearers, and the under-
signed."[19] There are German, Irish, and native volunteer
fire companies, who apparently forget fires in their
fights with each other.[20] If the Irish are a large part

---

[16]Thomson, Doesticks' Letters, p. 48.

[17]Thomson, Doesticks' Letters, p. 70, pp. 94-101.

[18]Thomson, Doesticks' Letters, p. 123.

[19]Thomson, Doesticks' Letters, pp. 80-81.

[20]Thomson, Doesticks' Letters, pp. 94-101. George
Foster, in New York Naked (New York: DeWitt and Davenport,
n.d.), pp. 125-133, says that volunteer fire companies
were of three types: regular volunteers, "sporting firemen" (i.e., gamblers), and fancy firemen (the Bowery
b'hoys). The b'hoys, according to Foster's contemporary
account, were all natives, had no visible means of support, and spent their time in stealing, fighting, and
stirring up trouble with immigrants. His description may
or may not contradict Constance Rourke's remark, in
American Humor (New York: Doubleday and Co., Inc., 1953),
that the Bowery b'hoys on stage are "undoubtedly Irish in
general ancestry." p. 116.

of the uproarious, sometimes dangerous life of New York,
they do not seem to be menacing, at least in this book.
They are simply an aspect of the colorful and fascinating
life of the city. Poverty, slums, noise, violence, and
civil strife--all the evils of urban concentrations--can
be laid to the Irish account; but this book seems more
interested in their vitality.

The Irish "National Character"

The presence in large numbers of Irish and other
immigrants drew a spate of commentary in the books on
the qualities of nations, the merits of immigration, and
the future of America. These comments frequently occur
in general terms, unconnected with characters and unre-
lated to plot; the temptation to generalize was apparently
very strong, and national character a favorite subject.
The opinions expressed on these questions offer a wide
range of conscious American attitudes toward immigrants
in general and toward the Irish in particular.

An Irishman is described in Catherine Maria Sedgwick's novel, Clarence, as "a compound of goodheartedness
and the absence of all principle," having "that mixture
of simplicity and cunning that characterizes his excitable
and imaginative nation."[21] The narrator of Scenes in the

---

[21]Sedgwick, Clarence, I, 87.

<u>Practice</u> <u>of</u> <u>a</u> <u>New</u> <u>York</u> <u>Surgeon</u> observes that "it is dif-
ficult to understand our Irish patients; so strangely as
the tragic and the comic seem to be combined in their
erratic natures."[22] This passage is a comment on the
attempted suicide of an Irishman; not even that can be
taken seriously. Cooper speaks of "the droll medley of
fun, shrewdness, and blundering, that is so often found in
the Irish peasant";[23] a character in <u>Florence</u> <u>DeLacey</u>,
moved by the acting of the original Tyrone Power, ex-
claims, "what a singular compound of fun, frolic, and
gentlemanly bearing, is a real Irishman . . . for even
among the lower orders, there is a natural ease and
politeness which removes them far from the clownishness
of ordinary rustics."[24] Much of the feeling behind these
generalizations seems to derive from traditional Irish
characters, rather than from observation. It is tempting
to see some greater accuracy in the remarks from <u>Clarence</u>,
harsh as they are, simply because of the empty conventionalism of Cooper and <u>Florence</u> <u>DeLacey</u>. These formulations
all agree, however, on irresponsibility and a kind of

---

[22]Dixon, <u>Scenes</u> <u>in</u> <u>the</u> <u>Practice</u>, pp. 22-23.

[23]James Fenimore Cooper, <u>Afloat</u> <u>and</u> <u>Ashore</u>; <u>or</u>, <u>The</u>
<u>Adventures</u> <u>of</u> <u>Miles</u> <u>Wallingford</u> (New York: Published for
the author and for sale by Burgess, Stringer and Co.,
1844), IV, 57.

[24]<u>Florence</u> <u>DeLacey</u>; <u>or</u>, <u>The</u> <u>Coquette</u> (New York:
E. Winchester, New World Press, n.d.), p. 44.

childishness as elements of the national character. Good
humor and politeness are simply the consequence, perhaps,
of a lack of seriousness.

Irish Politics

The American view of politics and political leaders
in Ireland is universally romantic and approving:

> Look at the glorious position of Ireland! where
> can you find moral grandeur to compare with
> it . . . ? A people trampled on for generations,
> and therefore ignorant and violent--a people
> proverbially impulsive, bold, and reckless,
> stand before the . . . British power, and say,
> as William Penn did . . . "Well, friend, thy
> strength shall never equal my patience."[25]

The occasion for this eulogy was the political policy of
Daniel O'Connell, and the temperance work of Father
Mathew.[26] The author of the violently anti-Catholic
Carlotina and the Sanfedisti praises the leaders of the
Young Ireland movement of 1848. He says of John Savage
that he "belongs to that bright constellation of Irish
patriots who are continuing in exile . . . the warfare

---

[25]Child, Letters From New York, p. 103.

[26]John Marsh, Hannah Hawkins, the Reformed Drunkard's
Daughter (New York: American Temperance Union, 1844) uses
a quotation from Father Mathew as an epigraph: "Temperance
is an oasis, a green spot in the desert of human life."
Father Theobald Mathew, a Capuchin priest, began a total
abstinence movement in Ireland in 1838. He met with great
success, spoke in England and Scotland in the 1840's, and
visited the United States in 1849-1851; in America more
than 500,000 took the pledge as a result of his work.

they commenced at home against oppression."[27]

These expressions of admiration for Irish political
behavior at home, in which the memory of American rebellion against Britain play a great part, do not extend to
the politics of the Irish immigrant. Irish in America,
according to these texts, did not have the same idealistic
tone. For example, the characters of Florence DeLacey,
continuing the conversation quoted above, praise the generosity of the Irish in the face of oppression, their
amiability, and their unwillingness to take vengeance;
but another character interrupts. "'And what the devil is
the reason,' exclaimed the elder DeLacey . . . 'that the
Irish, if they are such models of bravery, good-humor,
and politeness, all become Locofocos as soon as they land
upon our shores?'"[28] Another book darkly predicts that
in a few years America will be "a prowling wilderness--
peopled by nothing but Loco Focos and wild Irish."[29]

---

[27]Edmund Farrenc, Carlotina and the Sanfedisti; or,
A Night with the Jesuits at Rome (New York: John S. Tay-
lor, 1853), p. 390. He also praises Meagher, a speech by
whom is quoted at length, with admiration, by Sara Jane
Lippincott, Greenwood Leaves: A Collection of Sketches and
Letters. Second Series (Boston: Ticknor, Reed, and Fields,
1852), pp. 48-55. Another defense of Ireland against
British: George Lippard, Legends of Mexico (Philadelphia:
T. B. Peterson, 1847), p. 12.

[28]Florence DeLacey, p. 44.

[29]Catherine Read Williams, Annals of the Aristocracy:
being a series of Anecdotes of some of the Principal
Families of Rhode Island (Providence: B. T. Albro,
Printer, 1845), II, 33.

And a visitor to New York, contrasting politics there
with Southern customs, remarks:

> New-Yorkers never have what we call 'stump-
> speeches,' and never personally know, or even see
> their representatives. These city mobocracies,
> composed as they are, principally of wild Irish,
> are terrible things.[30]

This comment appeared in 1834, before the largest influx
of Irish; the same attitude is elaborated in a description
of a New York political rally, appearing in 1843. The
hall is full of Irish, German, French, and English immigrants, shouting and scuffling. The Irish, it seems, can
be identified because "the hair's all worn off their heads
a carrying brick hods on 'em."[31] Jonathan Slick, the
Yankee narrator of the piece, observes that "when the
people of these times sing out liberty, a feller can't
tell whether they mean to tear down a flour store or roast
a nigger alive."[32] Political appeals to immigrants are
the subject of several comic treatments. A balanced comment comes from Lydia Maria Child, who often expressed
a sane opinion:

> Political demagogues have aviled [sic] themselves
> of the influx of ignorant foreigners, to effect
> their own selfish purposes. As soon as an Irish-
> man lands, they pounce upon him, and urge him into

---

[30]William A. Caruthers, The Kentuckian in New York
(New York: Harper and Bros., 1834), I, 63.

[31]Stephens, High Life, p. 10.

[32]Stephens, High Life, p. 11.

citizenship and political action, whether he wishes it or not. The Irish hold the balance of power in this city, and their favor being much courted, corruption is the inevitable result.[33]

Reactions to the Immigrant

The passages above indicate uneasiness about the direction of American urban politics under the pressure of immigration in general. Irish are central elements of immigration, though other national groups are included. This uneasiness does develop, in various ways, into hostility; antagonism is shown in distaste for the immigrants' habits or appearance, in arguments for the slowing down or ending of immigration, and in Native American political activity. Examples of these abound in the texts, though the final judgment does not rest with the opponents of the immigrant.

Cooper, in a passage already quoted in connection with servants, regrets "the confusion of tongues that pervades the modern Babel";[34] again, looking back to the New York of 1800 with affection, he remembers "the beauty of the younger females . . . the true, native portion of

---

[33]Child, Letters From New York, p. 165. This letter, number XVIII, dated July 5, 1844, is a long and well balanced summary of Irish problems. See also, on immigrants and politics, Bickley, The Aristocrat, I, 114 and II, 158.

[34]James Fenimore Cooper, The Ways of the Hour. A Tale (New York: George P. Putnam, 1850), p. 89.

the population, and not the throng from Ireland and
Germany who now crowd the streets; and who . . . are not
in the least remarkable for personal charms."[35] Cooper's
characteristic nostalgia, and his consequent aversion to
immigrants on grounds which seem as much aesthetic as
political, lead to a bit of wishful thinking in Homeward
Bound;

> "So far from their [sic] being a desire to re-
> ceive rich rogues in America from other coun-
> tries, there is a growing indisposition to receive
> emigrants at all; for their number is getting
> to be an inconvenience to the native population."[36]

Doesticks was not especially favorable to the immigrants'
appearance either; he noticed "Dutch emigrants, with dirty
faces, nasty breeches, and long, loppy looking pipes;
Irish emigrants, with dirtier faces, nastier breeches,
and short, stubbier pipes."[37] And Edward Dixon spoke of
the "loathsome Irish neighbors" who occupied "the lower
apartments, almost in common with the pigs which were fed
from their very door-steps."[38]

But though the immigrant was not a pleasing part of
society, his presence could lead to more weighty objections.

---

[35]Cooper, Afloat and Ashore, II, 183.

[36]Cooper, Homeward Bound; or, The Chase. A Tale of
the Sea (Philadelphia: Carey, Lea and Blanchard, 1838),
II, 261.

[37]Thomson, Doesticks' Letters, p. 123.

[38]Dixon, Scenes in the Practice, p. 253.

Poverty among immigrants could cause social problems;
George Foster noted that of seventy thousand persons
receiving poor relief in New York all but fifty were
foreign-born and free negroes. The annual cost to the
city was put at two and a half million dollars.[39] Though
we have seen that the violence of the immigrant could be
treated lightly, the threat to public order remained, and
the Irishman could be described as "'an ignorant, unprincipled foreigner, who had no name and no stake in society,'" one of "'thousands of such men in the city, [who]
could be picked up anywhere, from the swarms about the
cathedral, to the dens of Catharine-lane.'"[40] The context
in this passage is the purchase of false testimony.

"A more improvident, heartless, and dishonest class
of people never defiled the fair face of the earth,"[41]
says Edward Dixon of the "low Catholic Irish." In the
light of attitudes like this, one can see that native
resentment might produce overt hostility. The threat of
retaliation is dramatically, theatrically expressed by
George Thompson:

> Have a care . . . for in the breasts of the
> American people there is a smouldering fire
> which may ere long break forth with terrific

---

[39]Foster, New York Naked, p. 116.

[40]Sedgwick, Clarence, I, 92.

[41]Dixon, Scenes in the Practice, p. 261.

fury and hurl destruction on the . . . hounds
that come . . . to feed and fatten on Yankee
abundance.[42]

Thompson's book, The Brazen Star, is the most violent
attack on the Irish in the sample; because its main character is Irish, it will be discussed more fully below.

Though the samples given seem to show strong feeling
against the Irish, the treatment given to Nativist movements in the books of the sample is not sympathetic.
A Protestant character in Pauline Seward, by John D.
Bryant, describing the Philadelphia riots of 1844, re-
counts how the members of the American Protestant Association were attacked by "a ruthless band of Trish Papists
. . . the national flag dishonoured by being torn in
shreds, and trampled under foot by a foreign rabble."[43]
The ultimate sympathies of the book, though not with the
Irish, are not with Protestants either, since the plot
concerns the conversion of the whole Seward family to
Catholicism. Thomas Nichols' Raffle for a Wife presents
nativists this way:

> "There is the whole Native American Corporation;
> they go for reform, every one of them. . . ."
> "They are opposed to foreign influence?"

---

[42]George Thompson, The Brazen Star; or, The Adventures of a New York M.P. (New York: George W. Hill, 1853),
p. 32.

[43]John Delavan Bryant, Pauline Seward; A Tale of Real
Life (Baltimore: John Murphy; Pittsburg: George Quigley;
Dublin: R. Grace and Sons, 1847), I, 191.

"Yes--death on the Pope, and down on the Irish. . . ."
"Your Native American Magistrate . . . turns a
German out of employment, and drives a score of
Irish apple-women from the walks around the
Park . . . and then publishes twenty thousand
copies of an English high tory book, which are
sent into every village in the country, to cor-
rupt the principles of our youth. . . . How many
Irish hod-carriers would have as much influence as
Allison, or the author of Ten Thousand a Year?"[44]

Nativism is also the butt of comedy. "Damn the

Native American Party!" says a drunken Irishman, "I could

whip 'em all." A Native American watchman suddenly

appears. "And indade," the Irishman says, "it was only

a bugbear I wanted to whip. It was no mankind at all,

at all."[45]

The son of an Irish immigrant comes home late, ex-

plaining, when asked, that he has been to a Native Amer-

ican meeting. His father gives him a thorough beating

for it. "'I don't care a copper for the flogging,' said

the juvenile patriot; 'but to be struck by a cursed for-

eigner is too bad.'"[46]

In Doesticks' Letters, a street preacher named

Gabriel lashes out at Rome, priests, and convents. An

Irishman in the crowd replies that heaven will consist of

potatoes, whisky, shillelaghs, and the absence of

---

[44]Thomas Low Nichols, Raffle For A Wife (New York:
Burgess, Stringer and Co., 1845), pp. 5-6.

[45]Child, Letters From New York, p. 164.

[46]Child, Letters From New York, p. 166.

Know-Nothings. After the fight, the Irishman is wheeled away in "his national carriage."[47]

Ray Allen Billington, in The Protestant Crusade: 1800-1860, mentions a preacher named John S. Orr, who called himself the "Angel Gabriel." During a visit to New York in 1854, Orr drew huge crowds, and the city had to provide an army of police to keep order because of his attacks on Catholics.[48] Billington also notes that "minor riots occurred in New York on nearly every Sunday in 1854, caused by street preachers and those who heckled them."[49] There is a great difference in perspective between Doesticks' rather li‑ht treatment of the subject and Billington's use of the word "riot"; the Irishman's bout with Gabriel may indeed fit the definition of riot, but there is no sense of crisis, the incident does not seem serious. It is simply one of those things that happen in the city.

None of the books in the sample take nativism--or the response to it--very seriously, except The Brazen Star. Whatever the strength of sentiment against the Irish expressed in these books, the alternative of nativist

---

[47]Thomson, Doesticks' Letters, p. 109.

[48]Ray Allen Billington, The Protestant Crusade: 1800-1860 (New York: The Macmillan Co., 1938), p. 306.

[49]Billington, Protestant Crusade, p. 319 (note).

activity does not seem to have been attractive.[50] Mrs.
Child sums up the general view: "Some of the means to
remove [Irish corruption] are neither liberal nor wise.
Banners with provoking and contemptuous mottoes, have
already given rise to a great deal of fighting. . . . If
ever the evil days of civil strife come upon us, we shall
find that these party processions and scornful banners
have sown seeds for a dangerous harvest."[51] The more
general American position on immigration—at least a position which could provide an image which makes immigration
a patriotic institution—is expressed in the following
passage, by George Lippard:

> The German and the Frenchman, the Swede and
> the Irishman, the Scot and the Englishman, met
> in the wild, and grouped around one altar—sacred
> to the majesty of God and the rights of man.[52]

This rhetorical description leads to a view almost completely contrary to the Nativist attitude of The Brazen
Star. It is not necessarily more truthful or responsible
as a description of the true American feelings; one can
imagine a man of the period responding to each in its
turn, in its context.

---

[50]Wright's exclusion of propaganda would reduce but
not eliminate Nativist sentiment.

[51]Child, Letters From New York, pp. 165-166.

[52]Lippard, Legends of Mexico, p. 15. Similar sentiments are in Samuel Hayes Elliott, The Sequel to Rolling
Ridge (Boston: Crocker and Brewster, 1844), pp. 15-16.

The attitudes toward Irish described so far have for the most part been drawn from formulations, verbalizations about the Irish. These verbalizations or judgments represent a range of ways in which authors or characters in books respond to Irish when they are thinking about them. That is, these bits of evidence reveal what people of the period said they thought about the Irish. The next sections of this chapter will examine material which may reveal what authors or their characters see in Irish when they are not thinking about them, but using them in books, casting them in roles, or visualizing their behavior.

Irish Roles

The most obvious and most important observation on the books in the sample is that in the large majority, Irish play no part at all. Although Irish are fairly numerous, and are spread through a large number of books, they seldom have any effect upon the events of the story. Their part is as detail, anecdote, background of the city. They do not apparently belong to the class of persons who can either help or hinder a hero in pursuit of his goals; in the ordinary course of events, Irish are simply not important enough in the minds of the authors to be cast in central roles.

The few stories in which they do operate prove the point. In T. S. Arthur's Sparing to Spend, an Irish

washerwoman who serves both the worthy Loftons and the
spendthrift Pinkertons helps along the plot by telling
young Pinkerton's fiancée about his unpaid laundry bill.[53]
In two books a respectable character is identified as
Irish by descent; but in both cases the Irishman came to
America at or before Revolutionary times.[54] Beyond these,
the Irish who are important in plots laid in the city
figure in books which have a special purpose.

A "fat, motherly Irish woman," Biddy McGee, together
with a German immigrant, cares for a crippled American
girl until her reluctant relatives can be made to take
her.[55] The point of this tale is the goodness and responsibility of the poor immigrant. The same point is made
in Daniel Mallory's story, "Curious Incidents." The narrator, traveling in Ireland on business, meets the parents
of Patrick Hogan. He reflects on the day in 1811 when
in spite of an aversion to hiring a green immigrant at
all, he hired Patrick because he looked and acted better

[53]T. S. Arthur, Sparing to Spend; or, The Loftons and
the Pinkertons (New York, 1853), p. 120. Bridget makes
several appearances.

[54]Cooper, Ways of the Hour, p. 56, Dr. McBrain's
grandfather was Irish; in T. S. Arthur, "The Fiery Trial,"
in The Ruined Family and Other Tales (Philadelphia: Godey
and M'Michael, 1843), the rich grandfather of a main character came from Ireland as a peddler.

[55]Russell, "Love's Labor Not Lost," Leaves From
Igdrasyl, p. 70.

than the other Irish.[56] Since Patrick Hogan had become
a trusted worker over the years, this story also seems
intended to prove the social usefulness of the immigrant.
It is also the only story with a city background to make
reference to the process of emigration, or to the families
at home.

Special interests are extremely evident in the only
two books which place Irish at the center of an entire
plot. The two span the spectrum of purpose and image in
their divergent ways. One is aimed at Irish Catholic
audiences, the other at Nativist prejudices.

Rosemary, by Jedediah V. Huntington, is a melodramatic tale of love, crime, intrigue, and marriage, set in
New York. Most of the principal characters are Irish,
and all of them are Catholic. Cahal O'Morra, a wealthy
New York lawyer, is the head of the family. His son,
Rory, graduate of a Jesuit college, is a medical student
in a New York hospital. In a discussion with a fellow
student, O'Callaghan, Rory explains that he is not Irish,
but a third-generation American.[57] He is thus the third

---

[56]Daniel Mallory, Short Stories and Reminiscences of
the Last Fifty Years. By an Old Traveller (New York:
Daniel Mallory, R. P. Bixby and Co.; Philadelphia: Carey
and Hart; Boston: Jordan and Co., 1842) II, 163-167.

[57]Jedediah V. Huntington, Rosemary; or, Life and
Death (New York, Boston, and Montreal: D. and J. Sadlier
and Co., 1860), p. 14.

major character to claim an emigrant grandfather; but
the O'Morras are thoroughly conscious of their Irish
affinities, as their names and their assertive Catholicism
suggest.

It is unnecessary to retell the story of Rosemary.
The plot is a tangle of kidnappings, rescues, near escapes, and confusion of motives. The significance of the
book is that it places Irish Catholics in the key roles
in a full scale romantic novel. It testifies to the
existence of an Irish professional elite, in the persons
of its characters; it testifies indirectly to the existence of an audience interested in such characters.
Rosemary is a Catholic novel, written by a convert, published by a Catholic house, aimed at a Catholic audience,
presumably; it is a bit unusual in that it is not defensive about religion nor interested in conversions.[58]

The other book with an Irish "hero" is at the opposite pole from Rosemary. George Thompson wrote The Brazen

[58]According to the Dictionary of American Biography,
Jedediah Vincent Huntingdon (Huntington in the text and in
Wright), 1815-1862, was of distinguished American ancestry. One grandfather served in the Continental Congress,
the other as a General. He earned an M.D. from Pennsylvania in 1838, became an Episcopal minister in 1841.
Stirred by the Oxford Movement, he first became High
Church, then a Catholic in 1849. He edited various
Catholic journals in the United States, and wrote novels,
often describing conversions. Rosemary, says the biogra-
pher, is regarded as his best book. See also the discussion of this book in Willard Thorp, "Catholic Novelists in
Defense of their Faith," Proceedings of The American Anti-
quarian Society, LXXV (1969), pp. 81-84.

Star in 1853, the year in which a uniformed police force
was instituted in New York City. The center of interest
is an Irish policeman, Dennis Finnegan from Cork, upon
whom Thompson pours rivers of abuse. He is described as
filthy, ugly, and uncouth; with hair like a scrub-brush,
a forehead half an inch high, eyes like decayed oysters,
a nose an enlarged pimple. His mouth is designed for
eating fish on Fridays.[59]

How Finnegan reached "the dignified and responsible
position in which we find him, is one of those . . .
unfathomable mysteries."[60] His disloyalty shows in his
hopes for an Irish President; "he believed in Daniel
O'Connell, and disbelieved in Daniel Webster."[61] His use
of authority is arbitrary and brutal. He never involves
himself with real crime, but rather arrests or harasses
innocent people. Half drunk all the time, he threatens
Dutch shopkeepers with arrest if they try to make him pay
his liquor bill. He takes bribes, protects brothels, and
never, ever, arrests an Irishman.

As an instance of Finnegan's police work, he captures
Larry Dolan with a load of stolen groceries meant for
Dolan's wife and children. Instead of taking Dolan in

---

[59]Thompson, The Brazen Star, pp. 21-24.

[60]Thompson, Brazen Star, p. 21.

[61]Thompson, Brazen Star, p. 22.

and returning the goods, Finnegan forces him to carry the groceries to the Finnegan home, and lets Dolan go.[62] The attack carries over to all Irish policemen; another one is described as driving children off the grass with "blows and curses," and striking an old woman, "the widow of a patriot who fought in the Revolution," for sitting under a tree.[63]

All of this is well within the range of possible attack on either Irish or policemen, however violent and overstated it may be. The curious aspect of the book is its main narrative line. Two native American policemen, Maxwell and Carlton, have been operating a large counterfeiting ring. Finnegan has been following Maxwell, watching him pass the counterfeit bills; when Maxwell passes the money in a clothing store, Finnegan catches him in the act. Oddly, the proprietor does not want to press charges, but has to acknowledge that Finnegan has the evidence. Maxwell pleads dramatically for his right to be arrested by an American, and not to have a foreigner humiliate him. This argument wins the sympathy of the crowd, and an American policeman is sent for. Maxwell therefore is taken away by his friend and colleague Carlton, swearing vengeance on Finnegan.

---

[62]Thompson, Brazen Star, pp. 28-29.

[63]Thompson, Brazen Star, p. 32.

From this point on, the story becomes hysterical in its vicious revenge on the poor Irishman. Carlton leads him to the counterfeiters' cave. The gang torments him, gleefully, and ignoring his pleas for a priest, they finally hang him. Presumably the absence of his testimony will bring Maxwell's release and lead to the marriage of Carlton to Maxwell's daughter.

There is a kind of madness about this set of values; Finnegan can do no right. He is equally guilty for committing crimes and for daring to capture a criminal. Maxwell, on the other hand, though a counterfeiter, is made to appear the victim of Finnegan's betrayal. If this attitude is to be taken at face value, the book seems to be hysterically Nativist, blind to everything except hatred for the foreigner, exploiting popular motivations wherever they can be found, and preaching explosive violence and murder. The book would be much more intelligible if it could be read as a satire on Nativist values, in ironic inversion.

Conventional Irish Traits

A large number of the characters in this group of city Irish are so sketchily described that it is not possible to assess their conventional marks in detail. The sole tag for many of them is the word Irish. Of course, the fact that this word seems to have been enough, without

examples of speech or other description, to categorize
the character, is evidence of the strength of the Irish
image. At the same time, it tells nothing about the content of that image.

The brogue is the most frequent indicator of the
Irish character. Irish characters speak in about half
the books, twenty of fifty-five. The most common indicators of peculiar Irish pronunciation are few: most common
is the vowel indicated by spake for speak, praste for
priest, craycher for creature. Also noted is pinny for
penny, till for tell, and timptation. Consonant changes
appear seldom, shown as murther for murder, shlape for
sleep, and wid for with. There is no definite pattern in
this except in the small number of sounds noted fairly
frequently. The first of the vowel changes, (spake for
speak) is also the most frequent point of pronunciation
found by Bartley in the period before 1800.[64]

A few words supposedly Irish in usage are found:
jewel, honey, and arrah among them, all noted by Bartley
as frequent in the plays of his sample.[65] Irish idioms,
like the use of "at all, at all," "sure and," and "don't

---

[64]J. O. Bartley, _Teague, Shenkin and Sawney_ (Cork,
1954), p. 282ff. Spake for speak occurs in 48 of 97
plays; pinny for penny in 12. The other points are not
noted.

[65]Bartley, _Teague_, p. 201; Arrah, 40 of 97 plays;
honey, 28; jewel in 20.

be after" are also used to mark an Irish speaker. These
indicators are all quite conventional; that is, the
speeches are marked by a small group of distinctive elements; the elements are familiar in literary tradition;
and they are (most clearly in the misuse of "after") not
derived from familiarity with actual Irish speech.

The associations of pigs, bogs, and shamrocks with
the Irish are notable by their almost complete absence;[66]
even the time-honored identification of the Irishman with
whisky is more evident in behavior than in phraseology.
Several Irish drink, a few are in the trade, but only one
book speaks of "that fabled panacea of all Irishmen."[67]
Shillelaghs come up twice; but the growing associations
are with wheelbarrows and hods. One new proverbial observation is the Irish dislike of Negroes.[68]

Names may indicate conventionality, besides revealing
something about the status of the character. More than
half of the seventy-eight Irish in this section have no
names given. Patrick and its variants is the name of
eight characters; Bridget of three, of the thirty-three
named characters.

---

[66]Pigs are mentioned only in Dixon, Scenes in the
Practice, p. 253.

[67]Isabel, p. 127.

[68]Oran the Outcast, II, 8; Stephens, High Life,
p. 11; Cooper, Homeward Bound, I, 175; Estelle Grant,
p. 209.

As for the traditional qualities attributed to Irish
in the British convention; the physical beauty of Irish
is not mentioned in this group of books. In fact, it is
reversed. Nor are there any references to Irish amorousness, or to fortune-hunting. The urban Irish in America
have lost these stage qualities. They do keep their reputation for fighting, though the quality of this has
changed. The older image of the Irish--which still
applies to the American image of the Irish in Ireland--
had a kind of grandeur about it, a flair for underdogs
and lost causes. The urban Irish fight in street brawls,
or channel their violence into crime.

The Irish fondness for whisky remains, though not
perhaps more marked than in the rest of the population.
The chief remaining conventional character is the freedom
and brashness of Irish manners. The urban Irish are not
at all abashed by authority, are quick to retort, and
demand their rights.

Bulls and blunders are uncommon in this group; only
in three books do Irish characters follow this pattern.
Only one of the bulls is worth repeating; a watchman wakes
an Irishman to tell him that the house is on fire. The
Irishman responds, "'By hoky, what do I care? . . . go

till the landlord—I'm only a lodger.'"[69]

In summary, the older British stage convention of the nationalized Irish character is much weakened in this sample of Irish in the American city. In many small ways the figure is simplified and redefined. Those dashing qualities that mark the convention of the stage have gone. So have the blundering comic traits of the Irish peasant and servant. The remaining elements are the brogue, with a few Irish signal phrases, a taste for violence, a cocky manner, a tendency to be called Paddy or Biddy, and a fondness for liquor.

Occupations and Status

There is evidence in the books for the occupations of about thirty of the seventy-eight Irish characters in this section. This of course implies neither that the rest are employed nor that they are not; many of the characters are simply encountered in the street, where their employment would not be of interest.

Six of the characters, all men, are driving some kind of vehicle—a coach, cart or dray. Three men carry hods or push wheelbarrows. Six men are policemen, guards, or watchmen; reference is made to firemen. Six more

---

[69]Frederick W. Thomas, Clinton Bradshaw; or, The Adventures of a Lawyer (Philadelphia: Carey, Lea and Blanchard, 1835), I, 243.

characters, four of them women, sell apples, oranges, flowers or cakes, from carts or stalls rather than in stores. These groups, which might be called peddlers, police and laborers, account for the bulk of Irish workers. Beyond these, three Irish (two of them women) rent out rooms, one keeps a bar, and one woman is a beggar.

All of these occupations are low in status, and all are apparently well down the economic ladder, though Finnegan's police work offers opportunities for graft. Even disregarding the indeterminate number of unemployed, this list presents the Irish as part of the pool of unskilled or semiskilled labor. They are not threatening native Americans in the economic sphere; they are not displacing Americans in desirable, high pay or high status occupations.

The very few characters who have higher status, or seem to, do not seem to upset the general rule. There is, for example, a young assistant in a lawyer's office; he might be a law student and therefore a future professional man, but he might also be an office boy, and the lawyer in question is anything but prosperous.[70] Two Irish characters are schoolteachers; one is a "professor of rhetoric" remembered rather comically by a former pupil.[71] The

---

[70]Stephens, Fashion and Famine, pp. 370-371.

[71]Stone, Ups and Downs, pp. 39-41.

other is headmaster of a school in Washington, praised as
"just, honest, patient," who is named and described with
such particularity that he is apparently based on an
actual person.[72] So, in Pauline Seward, the name of Hugh
Clair, an Irishman and "magistrate" involved in the
Nativist riots in Philadelphia, refers to an actual alder-
man.[73] If we take these two persons as real, the tendency
of imaginary Irish characters to have low status and low
income positions is very nearly an absolute rule, in these
urban plots. Only the O'Morras of Rosemary remain as the
exception. The literary Irishman is very probably far
less likely than the actual Irishman to be in business or
professional life.

Another question concerns the social or political
power available to the Irish characters. The political
commentary outlined earlier in this chapter makes it clear
that the Irish as a bloc were felt to have great political
power; but they were apparently obliged to turn it over to
native office-holders. There are no fictional mayors or
councilmen or leaders among the Irish. The only Irish
characters in this group who do hold actual power over
others are the policemen, most obviously of course in the

---

[72]George H. Throop, Lynde Weiss: An Autobiography
(Philadelphia: Lippincott, Grambo and Co., 1852), p. 88.

[73]Bryant, Pauline Seward, I, 192.

person of Finnegan. This sort of power, surely as exercised in The Brazen Star, is conceived as dangerous to other citizens, arbitrarily exercised, and undemocratic in its implications. The few other Irish policemen in the fiction are, however, mildly portrayed, so that Thompson's view of the menace is an isolated extreme.

Here again, as at almost every point, the characters of Rosemary are exceptions to the general Irish image. They do not speak in brogue, they are immune to the lower quirks of the national character, they are rich and independent, and have the political and social influence and contacts appropriate to their place.

Family Stability

There is little use made of family units in this group of books, and practically none at all of families as evidence of stability and responsibility (again with the exception of Rosemary). Three families appear as objects of charity: in none of these are both parents mentioned.[74] The Mysteries of Worcester presents an Irish family in a poor, crowded apartment, irritated and combative when a drunken American bursts in in the small hours, but finally kind and hospitable.[75] A group of Irish men,

---

[74]Oran, the Outcast, I, 104; Isabel, p. 127; Russell, Leaves from Igdrasyl, p. 39.

[75]Spofford, Mysteries of Worcester, p. 6.

women and children laughing and drinking on a coach, may be a family but scarcely argue for stability.[76]

The worst Irish families are in Stone's Ups and Downs, in which hatred, violence, and infidelity mark the tenements in which the hero lives.[77] Finnegan's family life is not very carefully explored, but his dangerous tendencies are clear.

The sole cases of constructive family relations are those mentioned in Arthur's Ruined Family, which deals with a remote emigrant, and Mallory's "Curious Incidents," which presents a family in Ireland.[78] In general, however, all the things a family can provide for a character--social standing, personal identity, influence, the promise of inheritance besides the education of the person in moral and social matters--are simply missing from the Irish pattern.

Religion

If the positive influence of family on Irish characters in these books is small, the positive contribution of religion is practically nil. The major use made of religion is its part in fomenting trouble between Irish and

---

[76]Ingraham, American Lounger, p. 40.

[77]Stone, Ups and Downs, pp. 171-182, 210-220.

[78]Arthur, "The Fiery Trial," The Ruined Family; Mallory, Short Stories, II, 163-167.

natives. Irish loyalty to their religion is strong, but although the authors do not especially condemn Catholicism, they do not show it as a spiritual influence on the Irish. No book in this group treats the relation between the Irish character and his church or his clergy.[79] Two books speak of Irish children in Protestant Sunday schools, which suggests that effective religious training might not be expected (in the image) in the context of their ordinary lives.[80] The recurrent protests of Irish Catholics and their bishops over the reading of the Protestant version of the Bible in the public schools is noted only once, and not stressed.

---

[79] A humorous exception: "If I thought she had settled her little reckoning with the priest, I should be happy to peruse her obituary." Said of an Irish character, in Parton, Fresh Leaves, p. 264.

[80] Isabel, p. 127; Parton, Fresh Leaves, p. 327.

IV. IRISH OUTSIDE THE CITIES

This chapter deals with the Irish characters who are
not servants and who are placed in settings outside of
urban areas. Books with characters of this kind are
scarcer than those with servants or with characters in
cities; the material for this chapter comes from only
about thirty-five books, compared to about fifty for each
of the others. There are some new elements in these rural
Irish, however, and in a few stories they are actually
the central characters.

The Irish in this section divide according to sec-
tional lines, both as to characteristics and to the type
of plot. Irish in the rural North and East are generally
used to demonstrate the possibility of successful assimilation; they are likely to have admirable traits. Irish
in the South are used to underline the evils of wage slavery and the heartless Northern treatment of immigrants.
Irish in the Southwest are almost purely comic. The sections will be the basis for the examination of the variety
of the rural Irish; but first we will examine Melville's
Irish hermit.

Oberlus

This Irishman, who appears in the ninth sketch of
"The Encantadas," is a fascinating portrait of viciousness
and squalor.[1] He is very probably the most complex and
interesting Irish character in the literature of the
period. His portrait is certainly not complimentary,
having none of the redeeming comedy of the type; still,
Melville is oddly reticent about the Irishness of Oberlus,
especially when his source is considered.

Much of the material in "The Encantadas" comes from
Melville's own observation, and the tone of the whole is
his. For the incidents in the history of the islands,
however, he drew from oral and written accounts. The
story of Patrick Watkins comes very largely from the work
of Captain Porter, who visited the Galapagos in 1813, some
few years after Watkins had left.[2] Other versions of the
story, some in print, existed,[3] but Melville confesses

---

[1]Herman Melville, The Piazza Tales (New York: Dix and
Edwards; London: Sampson Low, Son and Co., 1856), pp. 373-
391.

[2]David Porter, Journal of a Cruise Made to the
Pacific Ocean, by Captain David Porter, in the United
States Frigate Essex. 2d ed. (New York: Wiley and
Halsted, 1822), I, 131-135.

[3]Russell Thomas, "Melville's Use of Some Sources in
The Encantadas," American Literature, III (January, 1932),
433-435.

that he has followed Porter substantially, and often word
for word.[4]

The changes made from Porter's version to Melville's
are essential for an assessment of Melville's treatment of
the Irish type. Porter gives his Watkins red hair, and
has him growing potatoes. Watkins drinks heavily, and in
a central scene bullies and tries to enslave a Negro.
Porter's version of Watkins' letter says nothing about
British oppression; and he further adds a satirical para-
graph of speculation on the possible offspring of a "red-
haired wild Irishman" and a "copper-coloured mixt-blooded
squaw," the chief point (besides the ugliness of the children) being their unquestionable inheritance of the urge
to steal.[5] Porter has thus emphasized ugliness, filth,
theft, drunkenness, greed, insolence, and violence, and
connects these with Irishness. They seem as integral
a part of the character as the red hair, the potatoes,
and being called Patrick.

Melville's version of the story uses the red hair
and the potatoes, and keeps the story of Oberlus' laziness, filth, greed and violence practically as Porter
wrote it. The changes, however, seem significant. He has
reduced Porter's speculation on Watkins' descendants to

_____

[4]Melville, _Piazza Tales_, pp. 390-391.

[5]Porter, _Journal_, I, 134-135.

one sentence. In his version of Oberlus' letter,
Melville elevates the style into something resembling
traditional Irish verbal flourish, and adds the note of
suffering at the hands of England: "I am a patriot, exiled
from my country by the cruel hand of tyranny."[6] Most
important of all the changes is Melville's elimination of
any reference to Patrick Watkins' actual name; he even
changes Porter's "Pat's Landing" to "Oberlus's Landing."
These changes leave only indirect references to Oberlus's
nation; the word Irish is never used in the sketch.
Oberlus is described as "a wild white creature,"
a "European."[7]

Melville, presented with a complete sketch of a villainous Irishman in his source, has failed to exploit this
side of the material. Rather he seems to have taken some
pains to conceal it from plain view, and to introduce
a hint of more attractive aspect of the type in Oberlus's
letter. Considered in relation to the rest of the material in this section, this sketch remains complex and
mysterious; almost alone among the examples found, it has
no obvious political or social axe to grind, and no simply
conventional comic purpose.

---

[6]Melville, *Piazza Tales*, p. 388.

[7]Melville, *Piazza Tales*, p. 373.

<u>North</u> <u>and</u> <u>East</u>

Nearly twenty books display Irish characters in the
rural North and East. About half of these make very brief
appearances, and their traits and actions are well within
the limits of the traditional Irish figure derived from
the British usage. They show conventional marks in language, manners, and status, and the usual associations are
made.

The use of language by conventional Irish is marked
by the brogue, Irish idioms and catchwords, and blundering. In the nine books in which Irish appear very briefly,
five books give the characters a brogue; the other characters do not speak at all. A sample speech, which includes
brogue, idiom, and supposedly comic misuse of terms,
occurs in Harriet Beecher Stowe's <u>Uncle</u> <u>Sam's</u> <u>Emancipation</u>:
Irish maid Biddy, seeing a new cow, says, "Is it milking
that baste you'd have me be after?"[8] The humor of most
Irish speeches is small; apparently the fact that they are
Irish is expected to make jokes succeed. A young Irishman,
refusing to work on the Fourth of July, announces that
"I don't intind to lift a hoe the day; I'm in a free

---

[8]Harriet Beecher Stowe, <u>Uncle</u> <u>Sam's</u> <u>Emancipation</u>,
<u>Earthly</u> <u>Care</u> <u>and</u> <u>Heavenly</u> <u>Discipline</u>, <u>and</u> <u>Other</u> <u>Sketches</u>
(Philadelphia: Willis P. Hazard, 1853), p. 64.

country, and I'm able to support it."[9] The emphasis is
the author's, and the point of the joke is obscure. It
is apparently a speech blunder, but not a very ingenious
one. An oddly mixed description of Irish speech: "An
Irishman, in his uncouth national sounds, was most elo-
quently describing the death of Emmett," manages to cast
aspersions on the brogue while acknowledging the Irish
reputation for oratory.[10]

Speech oddities and blunders merge into odd behavior,
like that of the Irishman who swims into a purse-like
fishnet called a fyke, and nearly drowns. He comes up in
the net, and calls to his companion "as if he had found
a bird's nest: 'I say, Jimmy! be gorra here's a foike!'"[11]
Clumsiness and inefficiency also mark the Irishman; in
Susan Warner's The Hills of the Shatemuc an Irish porter
loses control of a wheelbarrow on a hill, and spills the
contents of a trunk.[12] In a misguided effort to show his
appreciation, Patrick Tatterdemalion, after getting food

---

[9]Sara Jane Lippincott, Greenwood Leaves: A Collection
of Sketches and Letters. By Grace Greenwood. Second Series
(Boston: Ticknor, Reed, and Fields, 1852), p. 249.

[10]Lydia Maria Child, The Coronal: A Collection of
Miscellaneous Pieces (Boston: Carter and Hendee, 1832),
p. 244.

[11]Frederick Swartwout Cozzens, The Sparrowgrass
Papers; or, Living in The Country (New York: Derby and
Jackson, 1853), p. 95.

[12]Susan Bogert Warner, The Hills of the Shatemuc
(New York: D. Appleton and Co., 1856), p. 161.

from a Protestant minister, blesses him in the name of
"all the saints in the Roman Catholic calendar."[13] We are
told that Irish must be supervised in doing simple garden-
ing work,[14] and that they break and train horses badly.[15]

Irish manners, besides being awkward, are likely to
be low. The Stage-Coach, like most of Lucius M. Sargent's
work, is temperance propaganda. In it an Irishwoman tells
her history; her first husband died of excessive whisky,
so she asked her second whether he drank whisky. He swore
he didn't; then he died of too much gin. The third swore
he drank neither, and perished from porter. The joke is
elaborated by her quoting Father O'Callaghan, who told her
it was all right to drink in self-defense, to keep the
wind off the stomach.[16] The village of Puddleford is
visited by a wandering Irishman and his wife, who perform
the Highland fling in full costume. "The Highlander was
drunk, and the woman was out of temper, the fiddle was

---

[13]Elhanan Winchester Reynolds, Records of the Bubbleton Parish (Boston: A. Tompkins and B. B. Mussey and Co.,
1854), p. 136.

[14]Stowe, Uncle Sam's, p. 62.

[15]Cozzens, Sparrowgrass, p. 95.

[16]Lucius Manlius Sargent, The Stage-Coach. Founded on
Fact (Boston: Whipple and Damrell; New York: Scofield and
Voorhies, 1839), pp. 199-210.

crazy, and the fife could scarcely squeak,"[17] but they

had six encores.

In this first group of characters, those who have

very brief roles in their appearances, all are low in

social status, so far as can be determined. Three are

simply described as laborers; others are a dairymaid,

a beggar, a thief,[18] and a pair of "wild Irishmen" who

have worked with horses. There are two instances suggest-

ing possibly higher status, namely a country hotelkeeper

and the musicians described above; but the hotel is noth-

ing more than a remodelled New Haven railroad car with its

"reception room" full of pigs,[19] and the musicians clearly

have no claim to skill or reputation.

All of the characters in this group show some of the

conventional marks, then, to some degree. None of the

characters shows any traits of speech, manner, or behavior

to contradict the accepted image. This seems to indicate

that there is not very sharp observation behind the use of

these characters. Irish may appear in these books because

[17]Henry Hiram Riley, The Puddleford Papers; or, Humors of the West (New York: Derby and Jackson; Cincinnati: H. W. Derby and Co., 1857), p. 281.

[18]Pascal Jones, My Uncle Hobson and I; or, Slashes at Life with a Free Broad-axe (New York: D. Appleton and Co., 1845). An episode tells how the narrator was robbed during a Millerite camp-meeting, by a character named McBowline; pp. 126-148.

[19]Frederic Townsend, Spiritual Visitors (New York: John S. Taylor, 1854), p. 79.

they actually do live in the rural North; but there is scant evidence that the authors had personal experience with them. At least, the characters show nothing that could not have been derived, almost in detail, from other books. This is so even though two of the books involved draw attention to Irish immigration as a social problem.[20]

In a second group of four books, Irish characters take a direct part in the action of the plot, or are developed at some length. In Sylvester Judd's Margaret, the title character, as an infant, is being taken on a long journey home. The party stay overnight in a shanty with an Irish family, good people who share what little they have with the travellers. The Irish wife nurses Margaret at her breast.[21] Though this episode is brief, it treats an Irish family, introducing a note of stable relation, though the portrayal is otherwise conventional.

One Irishman, the subject of a sketch in a travel book, diverges more strongly from the conventional pattern. Born in Ireland, he emigrated first to Philadelphia; then,

---

[20]Sargent, Stage-Coach, p. 199, says an Irishwoman's face possesses characteristics not to be mistaken, "whether we encounter them in the overpeopled cellars and garrets of a city, or upon their secondary migration to the far-away west." Reynolds, Records of Bubbleton, calls the Irish beggar "as voluble and resistless a scion of beggary as ever the heaving tides of emigration cast upon these afflicted shores." (p. 136).

[21]Sylvester Judd, Margaret: A Tale of the Real and Ideal, Blight and Bloom. Revised Edition (Boston: Phillips, Samson, and Co., 1857), I, 120. (First published in 1845).

as agent of a landowner, he went to Coudersport, Pennsylvania, in the thirties. At the time of writing of the
sketch (1855) he is a man of property himself, "one of
nature's nobility, an honest and a Christian man."[22]

"Little Bessie" is a sentimental story set in a New
England village.[23] Bessie, an orphan, is trying unsuc-
cessfully to collect the money due for sewing done by her
grandmother. The merchant who owes her the money is chat-
ting with the Deacon, and ignores her; the perfect image
of the indifference of commerce and religion. Hungry and
sad, Bessie leaves. Some friendly Irish laborers find
her, take her to Pat Reilly's for something to eat, and
send food home with her to her grandmother. They share
what they have with the unfortunate, even though "the
mouths at home are gaping like young swallows at Whitsun-
tide."[24] Irishness in this story seems to underline the
poverty of the workers, and to make stronger the point of
true charity found among the lowly.

Our Neighbourhood, a collection of tales and

---

[22]Samuel H. Hammond and L. W. Mansfield, Country
Margins and Rambles of a Journalist (New York: J. C.
Derby; Boston: Phillips, Samson and Co.; Cincinnati:
H. W. Derby, 1855), p. 344.

[23]Martha Russell, Leaves From the Tree Igdrasyl
(Boston: John P. Jewett; Cleveland: Jewett, Proctor, and
Worthington; New York: Sheldon, Lamport, and Blakenee,
1854), pp. 158-172.

[24]Russell, Leaves from Igdrasyl, p. 169.

observations on farm life in epistolary form, by Mary
Griffith, draws the figure of an Irish farm laborer.
Dennis is "excellent with the spade, and in the garden,
and with the wheelbarrow,[25] but he is also inefficient,
and unable to adjust to new situations. He is perfectly
willing to do monotonous work for long periods, work which
would bore anyone else; he seems not to have ingenuity or
imagination.

He is, however, extremely eager to please, and loves
to be praised. Consequently, he is liable to overdo
things.[26] He uses his day off to cut and carry blocks of
ice for the ice-house; he wants to be alone so no one can
catch him in a mistake. Mrs. Griffith remarks that "Of
all things, Irishmen dislike to be laughed at."[27] This
remark is an illumination; people must have expected
Irishmen to be funny, and to commit blunders as a matter
of course. A sensitive man would naturally be irritated.

Mrs. Griffith also observes, of slaughtering skills,
"I have never seen an Irishman that could prepare a hog
fit to be seen."[28] Irishmen love horses, but cannot learn

---

[25]Mary Griffith, Our Neighbourhood; or, Letters on
Horticultural and Natural Phenomena (New York: E. Bliss,
1831), p. 58.

[26]Griffith, Our Neighbourhood, p. 60.

[27]Griffith, Our Neighbourhood, p. 214.

[28]Griffith, Our Neighbourhood, p. 61.

to handle them properly.[29] Dennis' abilities and qualities compare unfavorably with those of Peter, a Negro
who works with him. Peter is good at everything; he is
intelligent, hardworking, inventive. "An American Negro
is one of the most useful of human beings,"[30] "better bred
and with better manners than whites of the same rank."[31]

This character sketch is interesting for many reasons. Dennis is treated recurrently in the book; he is
a present reality, and Mrs. Griffith has observed him
closely. He therefore seems quite believable and round;
he can surprise the reader. At the same time, lying
behind the observation, the conventional expectations and
judgments dictate many of the traits given him. Everybody
is waiting for him to be Irish; he must blunder, he must
be childishly dependent on praise, he cannot master machinery or improvise.

In general, the characters in this second group are
less rigidly conventional, and show more individual variation, than those in the first. They mostly have the
brogue, but blundering in speech or manners is less noticed (except in Dennis). There is no drinking, criminal-
ity, or irresponsibility; kindness, generosity and

---

[29]Griffith, _Our Neighbourhood_, p. 62.

[30]Griffith, _Our Neighbourhood_, p. 57.

[31]Griffith, _Our Neighbourhood_, p. 63.

sensitivity appear. There are added elements of stability; the characters have families in two instances, and one man is prosperous and respected. The characters have steady jobs, in three books at least. None of these people represents the slightest threat to the social order; if anything they are more responsive to others than natives are.

The third and final group of characters in the Northern and Eastern rural setting are the central characters of the stories in which they appear. There are five such plots, all short stories or tales, in three collections, all written by women. Each story is a demonstration of successful assimilation of the immigrant.

The life of Peter Mulroon, now "My Father's Head Farming-Man," in the story by Julia Mathews, is typical of this group of Irish characters. He landed in New York City in the 1830's. On his first day ashore, he met a girl from the next parish back in Ireland, now a house servant in a rich man's home. Later, when he went to visit her, he became lost in the maze of halls and rooms in the house. This was a lucky blunder, however, because he found the master's daughter in despair, helped her to elope, and as a result found himself working for the newlyweds. He married the Irish maid, of course, and rose to become the skilled and trusted superintendent of their farm.[32]

The conventional theme of the troubles of the raw immigrant is clearly worked out in this story; but it is made less conventional in effect by Mulroon's present position of stability and status. He has come a long way from being the blundering green Irishman who landed in New York nineteen years before, and can even take relish in telling the story (or perhaps embroidering on it). He is in no danger of being thought ignorant, clumsy, or childish.

Rose O'Neill was also born in Ireland. Orphaned at twelve, she was educated by her mother's uncle, an honest and sensible priest. She married Hugh Brady in Ireland just before the famine. She and Hugh emigrated to New York, where work was scarce. They went to Boston, where he worked on a railroad. Then, helped by an inheritance from relatives in Ireland, they bought a farm at Hazlehurst. They have made friends there, and have settled into a stable rural pattern of life.[33]

This is one of the very few stories to treat the

---

[32]Julia A. Mathews, "My Father's Head Farming-Man," in Lily Huson; or, Early Struggles 'Midst Continual Hope (New York: H. Long and Brother, cop. 1855), pp. 273ff. The story is told in the first person, in brogue, by Mulroon himself.

[33]Charlotte Ann Jerauld, "Rose Brady," in Poetry and Prose (Boston: A. Tompkins, 1850), pp. 398-416.

complete process of emigration, describing the life of
the characters on both continents with details of family
life and reasons for emigration. Still the struggle is
seen at a distance, from the perspective of present security, like the sufferings of the greenhorn Peter Mulroon.
The pains of the famine and of the crossing tend to be
minimized. The Bradys are drawn as sound, normal people,
who want to live a normal village life. Again almost
unique is the fact that their Irish families are both
known and respectable; even capable of leaving them money.
The stability of their family goes beyond husband and
wife.

A second story in the same book, "The Irish Daughter-
in-Law," describes anti-Irish prejudice in a New England
family.[34] Frank Channing, visiting in Ireland, marries
Eveline Beaufort (who is presumably Anglo-Irish or possibly upper-class native). Knowing that his mother and
sisters do not like Irish, he plots to win them over. He
sends Eveline home to work in the family as a (non-Irish)
governess; in a later letter he announces that he has
married "Bridget O'Brien."

The women respond as he knew they would. They are
sure the new wife is vulgar, and that she is "'tall, awkward, red-haired . . . fair and fat, with peony-hued

---

[34]Jerauld, Poetry and Prose, pp. 311-325.

cheeks and a rich brogue.'"[35] Though the father defends

the Irish, pointing to the heritage of Thomas Moore and

Robert Emmet, mother and daughters remain bitter.[36] They

are fond of Eveline, however, who has none of the charac-

teristics they assume are Irish; they express the wish

that Frank had married someone like her, instead of the

distasteful imaginary Irish girl. So all is resolved when

Frank arrives, and explains:

> "Had you dreamed that my sweet Eveline . . .
> was one of that luckless nation, your prejudices
> would have blinded you to her merits."[37]

This story, like the others in the group, is a tale

of relatively painless assimilation. Irish stereotypes

are openly raised and elaborated, but all break down when

applied to Eveline, who has none of the usual marks, not

even the brogue or an Irish name. She is, rather, pos-

sessed of breeding and family, and is quite eligible for

marriage. She is also quite far from the average Irish-

woman, at least of the emigrant class, and rather a spe-

cial case.

"The Irish Daughter," by Sara Jane Lippincott, de-

scribes the emigration of two Irish lovers, James Burke

---

[35]Jerauld, _Poetry and Prose_, p. 313.

[36]Jerauld, _Poetry and Prose_, p. 315.

[37]Jerauld, _Poetry and Prose_, p. 321.

and Mary Conway.[38] Separated by shipwreck, and united
again at the grave of Mary's brother, they marry and start
life again in America. "The Recognition and the Recom-
pense," a second story by Julia Mathews, describes the
fortunes of Mary Milton and her daughter Kathleen. The
narrator of the story had been saved by them after a shipwreck in Galway many years before; now he meets them in
the United States, newly emigrated, and on their way to
work on a farm near Philadelphia.[39]

The image of the Irish which comes out of this small
group of five stories moves farther from the conventional
limitations of the Irish. Marriage is now a central element; four of the stories have marriages as focal events,
and the fifth presents a mother and daughter. Three of
the marriages are Irish on both sides. Only in "The Irish
Daughter-in-Law" does an American marry an Irish girl, and
as we have seen, she is distinctly upper-class, not an
immigrant in the usual sense.

The strength of marriage and of family ties in these
stories is apparently meant to stabilize the image, and
place it solidly within normal American values. This stability minimizes the threat posed by the immigrant to the

---

[38]Sara Jane Lippincott, "The Irish Daughter," in
Greenwood Leaves: A Collection of Sketches and Letters.
By Grace Greenwood (Boston: Ticknor, Reed, and Fields,
1850), p. 129.

[39]Mathews, Lily Huson, p. 302.

social order. The same function is performed by showing Irish marrying Irish; this implies that immigrants will not disturb American social patterns by competing for American women.

Such disruptive elements of the Irish character as drinking and crime have completely disappeared in this group of stories. Even those traits which suggest childishness or irresponsibility are much less prominent. References to Catholic priests or practices are complimentary, again minimizing the possible threat to American ways. Much is made, on the other hand, of the aspects of the Irish image which elicit sympathy and admiration. The political struggle against England and the Irish reputation for eloquence and song are two such elements. Another is the pressure of the great potato famine, and the necessity to emigrate. Though emigration is prominent in these stories, it is not treated clinically, as the traumatic and dangerous journey it was. The physical and emotional stress of the passage is lessened in the stories by the passage of time; it seems like a necessary step toward the achievement of the promise of American life.

These evidences of selectivity indicate that this class of stories has a purpose: to demonstrate the success of the American system in handling the immigrant. According to this vision, existing institutions can readily accept the newcomer, who wants only to fit into the pattern.

The South

All but one of the ten books in this group were published after 1850; their authors are aware of the slavery controversy and of the mass immigration of Irish. Most of these books are a direct argument against the Northern books just discussed; whereas the Northern authors suggest that immigrants can be successfully absorbed into the system through Northern principles and practices, the Southern writers attack the North for imposing wage slavery on the immigrant, a bondage far worse than the chattel slavery of the South.[40]

Southerners cite the treatment given Irish servant girls in New England: "They're nothing but white niggers after all, these Irish," says the mistress, and accompanies the words with a beating.[41] And Irish laborers are

---

[40]See for example Vidi, Mr. Frank, The Underground Agent (Philadelphia: Lippincott, Grambo and Co., 1853), in which Jimmy O'Brien says that the Irish need more help than the Negroes, p. 113 (cited above, ch. III). Also see Emily Pearson, Cousin Franck's Household; or, Scenes in the Old Dominion (Boston: Upham, Ford, and Olmstead, 1853), in which a Northern woman suggests that the South eliminate slavery by hiring immigrants (p. 21).

[41]Mary H. Eastman, Aunt Phyllis' Cabin; or, Southern Life as it Is (Philadelphia: Lippincott, Grambo and Co., 1852), pp. 72-73. As the title indicates, this book is a response to the description of slavery in Uncle Tom's Cabin.

handled much the same. An Irishman is knocked down by
the superintendent of a railroad gang; he protests, "D--d
free country . . . I thought they only knocked niggers
over in Ameriky."[42] The superintendent explains himself:
"Railroads have to be made, and they have to be made the
right way. I aint afraid of the laws. I think no more of
knocking an Irishman over, sir, than I think of eating my
dinner."[43] It is suggested that Negroes are better off
than Irish, Scotch, or Germans; the Irish servant girl
has been wrenched from home and family, and has barely
survived the journey in the "packed cargo of emigrants."[44]
Compared with her pain, the Negroes on a well-run plantation are happy and prosperous.[45]

Francis Colburn Adams' Our World is the only anti-
slavery novel which uses Irish in a Southern setting. It
is a melodramatic book drawing for its effects upon all of
the horrors of slavery, including the sale of a white man.
Oddly, the book makes liberal use of Irish as villains.

---

[42]Eastman, Aunt Phyllis, p. 94.

[43]Eastman, Aunt Phyllis, p. 95.

[44]David Brown, The Planter; or, Thirteen Years in
the South. By A Northern Man (Philadelphia: H. Hooker,
1853), pp. 9-10.

[45]Brown, The Planter, p. 70.

> With the foreigner . . . affecting love of lib-
> erty at home . . . only makes him the greater
> tyrant when slavery gives him power to execute
> its inhuman trusts, . . .[46]

and the Irishmen in the book are brutal to the Negroes
under them. A native of Limerick, his face described
as "tyranny stereotyped," loves to whip his slaves;[47]
"General" O'Brodereque is a saloonkeeper and slave-
auctioneer;[48] Lawrence McFadden is an evil slaveowner,
crude in appearance, with broad face, low forehead, and
savage eyes.[49] Three Irishmen on a jury--James McNeilty,
Terrence McQuade, Patrick Hennessy--enliven the trial by
passing a bottle back and forth during the proceedings.[50]

The Irish in Our World are fairly strongly conventional in most of their traits, except that they are emphasized as brutal and disruptive, rather than comic.
They show the brogue, strongly Irish names, some of them
invented, drunkenness, violence, and an ironically in-
verted love of liberty. They are low in style and manner,
though some of them are more prosperous than the conventional Irishman. But high in such a vicious society is

---

[46]Francis Colburn Adams, Our World; or, The Slave-
holder's Daughter (New York and Auburn: Miller, Orton, and
Mulligan, 1855), p. 268.

[47]Adams, Our World, p. 3.

[48]Adams, Our World, p. 193.

[49]Adams, Our World, p. 268.

[50]Adams, Our World, p. 509.

low anyway. The intention may be to reflect adversely on Northern immigrants as well as on Southern slaveholders. The use of such crude Irish both destroys the amiable image of the plantation cultivated in the South, and implies that Irish will be undemocratic and vicious wherever they are found.

Three books, all by women, present what might be called a romantic image of the Irish character. E. D. E. N. Southworth's The Mother-in-Law takes place in Virginia.[51] The heroine is (of all names) Britannia O'Riley, descended from a landed Irish family, but in humble circumstances. When the story begins, she is a governess; she has no brogue but feigns one to annoy the lady of the house. She catches the eye of old General Stuart-Gordon, and marries him, thus becoming the mother-in-law of her best friend. It is a case of the bright, witty, poetic girl, temporarily out of luck, who rises back to her proper place, to the discomfort of those who snubbed her.

Britannia ("Brighty") has in fact high connections in Ireland; her cousin Frobisher, the Earl of Clonmacnois, comes to tell her she has inherited the family estate. He has many plans for it, including drainage, to improve the

---

[51]Emma Dorothy Eliza Nevitte Southworth, The Mother-in-Law: A Tale of Domestic Life (Philadelphia: T. B. Peterson and Brothers, cop. 1860). First published in 1851.

lot of her tenants. So Brighty renounces the estate in
his favor, like the sensible woman she is. She is Anglo-
Irish; most of the religious ceremonies are Episcopal,
though she jokes about becoming an abbess.[52] The presentation of the Irish character in this book is entirely
composed of high romance. To a lesser extent, the same is
true of Mrs. Southworth's The Curse of Clifton, which also
has an Irish heroine, not unlike Britannia, tucked away
in the West Virginia hills.[53]

Aaron Burr's adventure in the Mississippi Valley
began from an Irishman's island; naturally enough The Conspirators, a fictional version of the incident, includes
an Irish character. Eustace Fitzgerald (Blennerhasset) is
of a noble family, a "son of oppressed Erin," who has
built an elaborate mansion on an island in the Ohio
River.[54] He is "no degenerate son of that soil, whose
birthright seems to be wit, eloquence, and song."[55] He is

[52]Southworth, Mother-in-Law, p. 177.

[53]Southworth, The Curse of Clifton: A Tale of Expia-
tion and Redemption (Philadelphia: A. Hart, 1853).

[54]Eliza Ann Dupuy, The Conspirator (New York: D.
Appleton and Co.; Philadelphia: Geo. S. Appleton, 1850),
p. 1. The author's tolerant, even affectionate, treatment
of Fitzgerald, who seems to be a Catholic, is remarkable
in view of her violently anti-Catholic book, The Huguenot
Exiles (see below, ch. V, for a full account). She is
rather harsh in her treatment of Spanish Catholics in
The Conspirators also; Irishness seems to protect Fitzgerald.

[55]Dupuy, The Conspirator, p. 54.

treated as the innocent victim in the plotting. His
character is highly favorable; like Mrs. Southworth's
aristocrats, he displays markedly romantic Irish characteristics. This romantic character is of course highly
conventional, very little based on observation.

The only other books representing Irish in the South
involves a very brief look at a family descended from
an Irish soldier who fought in the revolution,[56] and a
story about emigration to the South.[57]

It is hard to see much more in the romantic treatments of the Irish than an instinct for the pleasing note
in building a hero or heroine. The characters are charm-
ing, dashing, witty; the note of romantic failure can be
touched. As for the first group, the motives are more
clearly visible. These books are part of the rhetoric of
the South.

The Southwest

Eight books contain Irish characters in Southwestern
settings; they are mainly travel books and collections of

---

[56]". . . you have enough Irish blood in you to make
the porker a necessary appendage to your family." Mary
Virginia Terhune, Nemesis (New York: Derby and Jackson,
1860), p. 19.

[57]Daniel Mallory, "Yellow Fever and Deer Hunt," in
Short Stories and Reminiscences of the Last Fifty Years.
By an Old Traveller (New York: Dan'l Mallory, R. P. Bixby
and Co.; Philadelphia: Carey and Hart; Boston: Jordan and
Co., 1842), II, 36.

humor. None of the Irish characters is central to the books, though some figure importantly in episodes. As is generally true for minor characters, comic characters, and characters not fully central, they tend to be conventional.

An Irishman may be brought in merely for a joke,[58] or, as in several books, for political satire. A well-digger at an 1848 campaign barbecue swears "that he had nivir heard of any Prisidint but Andhrew McJackson, and he meant to vote for him, dead or alive, as sure as swate Jasus was crucified."[59] The association between Irish and Jackson is strong in these books, and is the subject of much comic attention. In Mrs. Margaret Botsford's satire, The Reign of Reform, the porter at the White House is "an honest Pat . . . Mr. Jamie McFaddle O'Claugherty,"[60] an ignorant and corruptible hack. Jackson himself is represented as telling a Maine crowd that

---

[58]On falling off a cliff at (or into) Natchez-under-the-Hill, an Irishman cries, "That was a jewel of a lape!" Joseph Holt Ingraham, The South West. By a Yankee (New York: Harper and Brothers, 1835), II, 21.

[59]Joseph Cobb, Mississippi Scenes; or, Sketches of Southern and Western Life and Adventure (Philadelphia: A. Hart, 1851), p. 142.

[60]Margaret Botsford, The Reign of Reform; or, Yankee Doodle Court (Baltimore: Printed for the Authoress, 1830), p. 64.

"though I tell'd em down south my father was
an Irishman, and my mother, too, I am as clear
a Yankee as the Major himself."[61]

South in this case apparently means New York; but at any
rate Jackson seems to carry the Southwest with him wherever he goes. In William Price's Clement Falconer, significantly subtitled Memoirs of a Young Whig, several
Irish characters appear, two of them rabid Jacksonians.
Terence McGrath, editor of a Kentucky newspaper, who has
been in his day horsewhipped for printing libels, is seek-
ing the consolation of a post-office as a reward for his
services to Jackson.[62] The other Jacksonian is an Ulster
Irishman from Pennsylvania. The controversy over the
Ulsterman--whether he should be characterized as Irish or
Scottish--is beyond the scope of this study. Still, as
Brackenridge suggested, the western mountains were "half
Ireland";[63] and the people were chiefly from the North,
not "aboriginal Irish." Jackson's father came from the
North of Ireland also. It is therefore odd that the
native Irishman, the Irishman of the brogue, who swears by

---

[61]Charles Augustus Davis, Letters of J. Downing,
Major, Downingville Militia, Second Brigade, to his Old
Friend, Mr. Dwight, of the New-York Advertiser (New York:
Harper and Brothers, 1834), p. 251.

[62]William Price, Clement Falconer; or, The Memoirs of
a Young Whig (Baltimore: N. Hickman, 1838), I, 13. The
other Irish are a maid and an habitual petitioner of
Congress.

[63]Hugh Henry Brackenridge, Modern Chivalry, ed. Claude
M. Newlin (New York: American Book Co., 1937), p. 405.

"swate Jasus," should be taken into the Southwestern
Jacksonian image. Very probably the answer is that there
was no ready conventional image for the Ulsterman, while
the "aboriginal" image was available.

The preceding books form a unit which uses the Irish
character to score satirical points against the Democrats.
Willard Thorp, discussing the point of view in Southwest
humor, has drawn attention to the political dimension of
the satire: "It permitted him, if he was a Whig--and he
usually was--to dissent subtly from the 'Democratic' behavior of his characters."[64] The ignorant and partisan
Irishman can be used to discredit the party.

Without the political satire, but in the same general
type, is the Irishman Mulrooney, a well-digger in Missouri,
caught passing a counterfeit dollar. Pursued, he fights
with everything he can reach--bottles, club, and pistol.[65]
More criminal and violent is a convicted kidnapper described by Charles Sealsfield:

> . . . the most repulsive . . . churlish, obdu-
> rate, malicious physiognomy, with a dark, fiendish,

---

[64]Willard Thorp, _American Humorists_ (Minneapolis:
University of Minnesota Press, 1964), p. 13. The same
point is made in Frank Baldanza, _Mark Twain: An Introduction and Interpretation_ (New York: Holt, Rinehart and
Winston, 1961), p. 25.

[65]John Beauchamp Jones, _Life and Adventures of a
Country Merchant_ (Philadelphia: Lippincott, Grambo and
Co., 1854), pp. 45-49.

and sneering expression. . . . It could be seen
at once that he was an Irishman.[66]

Sealsfield (Karl Anton Postl), a naturalized citizen who
returned to Europe after nine years in America, remarks
that the laws of the United States are so mild that "even
this foreign scoundrel" will receive a short prison sentence. Postl's further journeys in the West led him to
cities populated by "Irish, and Scotch, and Germans, and
French";[67] America thinks "no child of Adam, whether
German or French, Irish or Russian, unworthy of its
kindness."[68]

The low, sometimes violent, image of the Irish character is further exemplified in the most fully presented
character in the group, a Texan woman in a tale by Charles
W. Webber. Aunt Beck, half Scotch and half Irish, went to
Texas with Austin. Her husband had become an outlaw,
together with six of her sons. The husband killed the
seventh son, whereupon Aunt Beck killed him and drove
the rest of the sons away.[69] She now keeps a tavern,

---

[66]Charles Sealsfield (Karl Anton Postl), Life in the
New World; or Sketches of American Society (New York:
J. Winchester, New World Press, 1844), p. 28. The inci-
dent takes place in Mississippi.

[67]Postl, Life in the New World, p. 179.

[68]Postl, Life in the New World, p. 180. A bad Irish
bull is on p. 79.

[69]Charles Wilkins Webber, "The Texan Virago and the
Tailor of Gotham," in Tales of the Southern Border (Philadelphia: Lippincott, Grambo and Co., 1853), p. 126.

and carries on a bit of smuggling. The priests are said
to protect her, because she was educated as a Catholic,
and is generous to the Church. Unprincipled and violent
as she is, she has made religious pilgrimages to a shrine
at Monterey. Her part in the actual tale is benevolent
and comic; the story concerns a practical joke played on
a tenderfoot from New York.

Aunt Beck seems to be dominantly Irish, because of
her religion and her style, but the author takes her mixed
parentage seriously. Her speech is an odd alternation of
Scottish and Irish elements: "'Sure and yes, hinny! Ye
should be afther ateing enough;'" "'Ah, chiel Dicky! chiel
Dicky! ye're ower brash!'" These two examples are from
the same page.[70]

The Irish image which emerges from these Southwestern
associations is markedly limited to certain possibilities.
It is comic, politically ignorant and fanatical, violent
and unstable. It resembles the style of the first group
of Northern Irish, though the note of crime and violence
is much stronger here. None of the stability of the
Northern stories of assimilation appears at all. Nor does
any of the romance of some of the Southern versions of
the Irish have any parallel in the Southwest.

Marriage and family ties are virtually non-existent.

---

[70]Webber, Tales of the Southern Border, p. 137.

Only Aunt Beck is given a family history (excepting
Andrew Jackson), and her family is criminal, unstable,
and marked by bloody violence. All of the characters
are socially and economically low. A newspaper editor
is perhaps the highest in status, but the paper in question is characterized as a political scandal sheet.

Behind the veneer of comedy, the Irishman in the
Southwest is an unstable character, without personal ties
to order, without effective religious standards, and completely without an economic stake in society. The implications of the character are therefore threatening;
whether in the Irish character in itself, or in the Irishman as symbol of levelling democracy, the possibilities
for the disruption of society are many.

V. IRISH RELIGION AND THE CATHOLIC CHURCH

Irish immigrants were an increasingly important part
of the Church in America during the period under study.
It would therefore seem logical that the Irish character
would be closely linked with Catholicism in the fiction;
but the relation is not as close as might be expected.
It is true that most Irish are expected to be Catholic,
but a great number of the most important Catholic characters are not Irish. Furthermore, Irish do not even appear
in most books in which Catholicism is a central theme.
Irish religion is a separate theme from the fiction of
the Catholic Church; the wide differences in tone and
treatment between the two help to underline some important
aspects of the Irish image.

The Catholic Church

A constant stream of incidents and controversies kept
the Catholic Church in the forefront of American minds,
starting with the Quebec Act. Ray Allen Billington has
outlined them; briefly, the incidents during the period
were these.[1] The quarrel between Bishop Conwell of

---

[1]Ray Allen Billington, The Protestant Crusade: 1800-
1860 (New York: The Macmillan Co., 1938), pp. 16-20, 37-48.

Philadelphia and the Trustees of St. Mary's Church produced a minor schism and strong reaction from outside the Church. The debate over Catholic Emancipation in England brought on the publication of floods of anti-Catholic material, and much of this was imported into the United States. Leo XII held a Jubilee in 1827; the bishops of the United States met in the First Provincial Council of Baltimore in 1829. Both events provoked Protestant antagonism. So of course did the controversies over reading of the King James Bible in the public schools during the next fifteen years. The burning of the Mount Benedict convent and the riots in Kensington in 1844 were evidence of the intensity of feelings on both sides. Perhaps the crowning event in the sequence was the behavior of Pius IX; hailed as a liberal at his accession, he was ruthless in suppressing the liberal movements in 1848. In the midst of change all over Europe, he made himself into an image of absolutism and dogmatic certainty, an image further perfected by his Syllabus of Errors in 1854. At this point, the Catholic Church seemed to confirm the worst caricatures of itself, negating the intellectual and liberal image which had been developing.

For there was an alternative view of the Church, represented in England by John Henry Newman and in the United States by Orestes Brownson. The Church of Newman

was surely intellectually respectable, a traditional home
of the spirit. It was socially respectable as well,
stable, scholarly and relaxed.

Both versions of the Church have found their way into
the fiction in the sample. It is plain that the Church of
Newman and Brownson is far less interesting as a fictional
topic than the oppressive Church of mystery and power.
That Church is strongly identified in the fiction with
France, Spain, and Italy, and will be dealt with first.
The Church in Colonial America is a milder affair, espe-
cially in the West; and the Church in the United States is
seldom treated with any of the horror so common in
European settings.

The Church in France and Italy

Ever since Matthew Lewis' The Monk, the fictional
image of the Catholic Church was associated with mystery
and sinister power, in the kind of plot identified as
Gothic.[2] The essential ingredient of this plot is the
presence of arbitrary power, of a kind of privilege which
runs over the rights of the individual. The Gothic con-
frontation, in this definition, is between the individual
seeking happiness and the institution which holds him in
its power. The predicament is at bottom as much political

---

[2]Matthew G. Lewis, The Monk: A Romance (London:
J. Bell, 1796).

as it is religious; the misuse of privilege.

An example of the Gothic thus defined is Eliza Ann Dupuy's The Huguenot Exiles.[3] The central character is a vicious priest. Father Antoine's rooms are an image of himself. His library, with its massive bookcases, religious paintings, jewel-encrusted missals, and emerald rosary, bears witness to wealth and to an excellent (though baroque) taste for knowledge and beauty. His bedroom is bare except for a simple pallet, a crucifix, and a skull and crossbones; it symbolizes his celibate simplicity and discipline. The two rooms show the visible face of his Church, simultaneously rich, cultured, and ascetic.

Behind the bedroom, however, a secret panel opens into another apartment, this one hung with silks and erotic paintings, where Father Antoine gratifies the sensual appetites suppressed in his public life.[4] He claims to have bought the right (from the Pope) to enjoy these luxuries.[5] This room supplies what the public rooms lack; they showed cold power with self-denial, while his hidden room explains all in the drive of lust.

The plot is set in seventeenth century France, during

---

[3]Eliza Ann Dupuy, The Huguenot Exiles; or, The Times of Louis XIV (New York: Harper and Brothers, 1856).

[4]Dupuy, Huguenot, pp. 77-78.

[5]Dupuy, Huguenot, pp. 79, 327, 414.

the persecution of the Huguenots. The father of the
heroine has just died; Father Antoine, alleging heretical
tendencies in the family, puts both Eugenia Altenburg and
her mother in a convent. Mme. Altenburg dies, probably
of poison,[6] and Eugenia is pressed to join the sisterhood.
Should she become a nun, her property would belong to
the Church, and she herself would be in the power of
Antoine. She recoils at the last moment, at the point of
making her final vows and the symbolic cutting of her
hair;[7] and though she is sentenced to three days in total
darkness in a cave beneath the convent, she is rescued by
her lover. Both ᠭo into exile with the Protestants.

Father Antoine, as the representative of the Church,
embodies a number of European attributes against which the
American mind reacts; he stands for entrenched traditional
authority, backed by an ancient institution, against which
the individual is helpless. He is the beneficiary of a
secret power structure, which dispenses favors to the
loyal. He can steal and punish with impunity;[8] and most
Gothic horror of all, he can work his will on women,
through the convent. The perfect occasion for extracting
all of the pathos and horror from this image is the

[6]Dupuy, Huguenot, p. 238.

[7]Dupuy, Huguenot, p. 420.

[8]Dupuy, Huguenot, p. 56.

pursuit of a beautiful young virgin by this powerful,
unscrupulous priest.

Three bits of machinery are important emotional stim-
ulants in this book, and carry over into others of the
type. They are confession, the convent, and the Inquisition. Of the institutional patterns of the Church, these
are the most persistent in plots of this kind, because
they best exemplify the kind of power involved.

Father Antoine is Eugenia's confessor while she is
in the convent. Since she was young and pure, with no
real sins to confess, she "commenced laying bare the im-
pulses and emotions of her own heart." As a result, the
priest "held in his hand the clew to every impulse of
that inner life he was so anxious to influence."[9] The
confessional is a better tool for domination than spies,
for the victim comes voluntarily. The evil man can turn
everything to his own ends.

The convent is another of the priest's weapons. Like
the confessional (and like his rooms) it turns a good side
to the public. Eugenia does not learn the true nature of
life in the convent while she is a novice; only after she
has taken her vows will the nuns tell her about the
orgies.[10] At that point she would be bound to the convent,

---

[9]Dupuy, Huguenot, p. 332.

[10]Dupuy, Huguenot, p. 326.

supposedly, by all force of law, and no escape would be possible.

The form the law takes in the book is the Inquisition. In the cellars of the convent there is

> a circular room, lighted by lamps, shaded . . .
> to afford a ghastly light. . . . On the walls
> were painted scenes from purgatory, and wretched
> beings were undergoing every species of torment
> the imagination of fiends could invent. . . .
> Against the wall . . . opposite the entrance,
> was the seat of the inquisitors. . . . Above their
> heads hung a picture of Thomas Aquinas, whose
> intolerant doctrines are held in extreme rever-
> ence by the most uncompromising portion of the
> believers in Rome. . . . His chief dogma, "Death
> to all heretics," renders him particularly accept-
> able to the inquisitors.[11]

Here Eugenia is condemned to her three days in the cave, followed by life imprisonment.

This ominous court, quite unnecessarily (but color-fully) hidden away in a tomb, is the final bulwark against the individual. A purely literal and technical law is applied by the system, in favor of the system. Justice is out of the question.[12]

The actions of Father Antoine and his followers in the rest of the book fill out the combination of personal

---

[11]Dupuy, Huguenot, p. 308.

[12]As a matter of fact, none of the machinery employed against Eugenia is legal under the Code of Canon Law as published in 1917. Physical violence renders vows taken under fear invalid, according to Canon 103. Presence of grave or unjust fear makes profession in religion invalid, according to Canon 572, sec. 1. This is not to say that the law stood thus in those times, nor that a law cannot be perverted.

lust and political repression. His agents torment the Huguenots in their worship, destroy their property,[13] and take away their children.[14] The children are taught to obey the Church, to avoid the Bible, and to forget their parents. Here again, heartless "European" values are drawn to contrast with American, Romantic, and Protestant ideals.

The popularity of this type of imagery about the Catholic Church is shown by the number of similar plots. Two books are set in the arena of fourteenth century Italy; the problem is the political conflict among Popes, Hungarians, and Italians for power in Naples. In Joanna of Naples, the priest's role is mainly political intrigue; in The Catanese the priest tries to seduce a fisherman's daughter.[15] In Carlotina and The Sanfedisti, set in the Italian uprisings of 1848, politics and lust are mixed about equally; Father Francisco lives in a room like

---

[13]Dupuy, Huguenot, pp. 74-75.

[14]Dupuy, Huguenot, pp. 385-388.

[15]Louisa Jane Hall, Miriam; and, Joanna of Naples (Boston: Wm. Crosby and H. P. Nichols, 1850); Ella Rodman Church, The Catanese; or, The Real and The Ideal (New York: Bunnell and Price, 1853).
Joanna is especially interesting in the way it alters the historical context to suggest that Joanna is the heroine of a nationalist movement against Hungarian intervention, which is pushed by the Pope. The facts seem to have been that Joanna was trying to play off the French against the Hungarians, and helped elect a Pope of her own to complicate things.

Antoine's, surrounded by symbols of death, pictures of hell, and instruments of self-discipline.[16] Father Ambrose, in Theodore Sedgwick Fay's Norman Leslie, is purely lustful. He uses the confessional and his priestly office to press his suit.[17]

These novels of the Church in Latin Europe use the Church as a symbol of reaction and repression. Priests and kings, supported by the vested interests, conspire to suppress liberty of thought and action in favor of dogma and absolutism. Privately, both priests and nobles seek gratification from the women in their power. The machinery of the tales involves symbols of death, burial, and decay, imprisonment and suffering; it is the machinery of the Gothic.[18]

---

[16]Edmund Farrenc, Carlotina and the Sanfedisti; or, A Night with the Jesuits at Rome (New York: John S. Taylor, 1853).

[17]Theodore Sedgwick Fay, Norman Leslie. A Tale of the Present Times (New York: Harper and Bros., 1835), II, 63.

[18]Another Huguenot story, without a strong priest figure, is Mary Jane Windle, "The Huguenots," Truth and Fancy: Tales Legendary, Historic, and Descriptive (Philadelphia: C. Sherman, Printer, 1850).
Three other books deal with Southern Europe less intensely, using some of the same material with merely exotic interest: Nathaniel Parker Willis, Inklings of Adventure (New York and London: Saunders and Otley, 1836) notes mummies of monks in Sicily, p. 206; Henry Theodore Tuckerman, Isabel; or, Sicily (Philadelphia: Lea and Blanchard, 1839) has a girl entering convent, with cutting of hair, p. 119; Humorist Tales (New York: Nafis and Cornish; St. Louis: Nafis, Cornish and Co., cop. 1841) has a brief narrative of village life with a mild priest.
Two books only deal with the rest of Europe; The Polish

Colonial America

The priest in France is a powerful and terrible man;
but the French priest as a missionary in the American West
is gentle and benevolent. Jesuits in Europe are vicious
schemers, but Jesuits or Franciscans in Wisconsin are
idealized figures. Every mention of these priests is
favorable.[19]

This fact is a striking demonstration of the effect
of context on the character type. In the American West,
the priest is not the agent of a highly organized institution, but a solitary man of peace, physically helpless.
His antagonists are not European Protestants or liberals,
but Indians, possibly hostile. As a Frenchman, he does
not seem to present a threat to the American movement,
as the English did; and to a locality seeking a history,

Chiefs: An Historical Romance (New York: J. K. Porter,
1832) tells a story about Kosciusko's love for a girl who
later became a nun; there is no Gothic or hostile treatment. Julia Mathews, Lily Huson; or, Early Struggles
'Midst Continual Hope (New York: H. Long and Brother,
cop. 1855) has a colorless scene in England.

[19]References occur in James Hall, The Wilderness and
the War Path (New York: Wiley and Putnam, 1846), p.117ff.;
Henry William Herbert, The Chevaliers of France from the
Crusaders to the Marechals of Louis XIV (New York: Red-
field, 1853), a Jesuit missionary, p. 309ff.; Remarkable
Narrative of the Female Hermit. And Teloula, The Indian
Girl (Boston, 1849), p. 24ff.; Henry Hiram Riley, The
Puddleford Papers; or, Humors of the West (New York: Derby
and Jackson; Cincinnati: H. W. Derby and Co., 1857),
p. 210; Lydia Maria Child, "The Recluse of the Lake," The
Coronal: A Collection of Miscellaneous Pieces (Boston:
Carter and Hendee, 1832), p. 91; also Child, "The Indian
Wife," The Coronal, pp. 171-172.

the French past provides a kind of pastoral and romantic
image. For all of these reasons, the French explorers
and missionaries of the Middle West are presented as holy
and benevolent men.

The Spanish colonies are generally presented as
romantic and exotic. Not very much Catholic material
appears, and such as there is is quaint and harmless.[20]
The Mexican War provides a few scenes of pathos, such as
one of nuns killed while at prayer.[21] One novel has its
climax in a convent in Havana, with the criminals dis-
guised as priests; but the convent had been used by her
relatives to hide the heroine, and none of the Gothic
aspects of the Church are exploited.[22]

The most extensive treatment of the Spanish terri-
tories is given in The Conspirator, another novel by Eliza
Ann Dupuy, which relates Aaron Burr's attempt to seize

---

[20]Examples occur in James Fenimore Cooper, Afloat and
Ashore; or, The Adventures of Miles Wallingford (Philadel-
phia: Pub. by the Author, 1844), II, 183-184; William
Henry Herbert, Tales of the Spanish Seas (New York: Bur-
gess, Stringer and Co., 1847), p. 26; George Lippard,
Legends of Mexico (Philadelphia: T. B. Peterson, 1847);
J. R. McDowell, Henry Wallace; or, The Victim of Lottery
Gambling (New York: Wilson and Swain, 1832), p. 89; Herman
Melville, The Piazza Tales (New York: Dix and Edwards;
London: Sampson Low, Son, and Co., 1856).

[21]Sara Jane Lippincott, Greenwood Leaves: A Collection of Sketches and Letters. Second Series (Boston:
Ticknor, Reed, and Fields, 1852), p. 109.

[22]McDowell, Henry Wallace, pp. 89-92.

the West.[23] The bishop of New Orleans is active in the political maneuvering; it is said that he can move the people to whatever he wishes, and that he intends to destroy any attachment to the United States. The strongest Catholic character in the book, however, is a nun. Inez Zavala, the heroine, enters the convent after an unhappy love affair. The Mother Superior, who had entered for the same reason, wants to marry Inez to her nephew, to cement a family alliance and bring her own family back into prominence. "Power, place, and wealth . . . what is existence without them?" she asks her startled nephew; she tells him she could have ranked with Elizabeth of England and Catherine of Russia, if her male relatives had not made political blunders.[24]

This convent is free of sexual irregularity. Inez is subjected to rigid discipline in spirituality; forced to spend hours in prayer for "indulging the feelings which bind us to earth," she asks herself "Must I subdue myself into a mere automaton before I am worthy to call myself his follower?"[25] The whole tone of the Church is altered between this book and The Huguenot Exiles. Though the Church in The Conspirator has power over people, and

[23]E. A. Dupuy, The Conspirator (New York: D. Appleton and Co.; Philadelphia: Geo. S. Appleton, 1850).

[24]Dupuy, Conspirator, p. 209.

[25]Dupuy, Conspirator, p. 207.

exercises political influence, it is not the violently brutal and repressive Church of The Huguenot Exiles. The difference in context once again has affected the style of the image, this time in two works by the same author.

It is only in the British colonies that the Gothic Church appears. John Lothrop Motley's Merry-Mount presents a curious Catholic character, Sir Christopher Gardiner. The report of his life is that he has been a Knight of Malta, married, put away his wife in order to become a Cardinal, and failed of election as Pope by a single vote. He then went East, became a Moslem, and fought for the Sultan. His true history is less spectacular, though some of the elements are the same. His real name is Fulk de Gorges; he was a Knight of Malta, took two wives, contrary to his vow of celibacy, and was forced to flee and change his name. The rumor implied the more Gothic view, that the Church condoned or rewarded at least some of his crimes, while the true story does not. In any case, he is the agent of the Stuart King, whose cause was linked with Catholicism, and his capacity for intrigue and deceit is high.[26]

The Catholic villain of Hansford, by St. George Tucker, has learned his evil ways directly from the Church.

---

[26]John Lothrop Motley, Merry-Mount: A Romance of the Massachusetts Colony (Boston and Cambridge: James Munroe and Co., 1849), pp. 71-72.

"Good Father Bellini," he muses, "thou has taught me true
wisdom; 'Success sanctifies sin.'"[27]   He also quotes
St. Ignatius Loyola to justify lying. After adventures
in Virginia, he returns to England, where he takes part
in one of the Popish Plots and is imprisoned, "true to
his religion if to naught else."[28]

Two Colonial novels use the confessional as a plot
device, though in both cases the supposed priest is a lay-
man in disguise. In Emerson Bennett's Rosalie Dupont,
an American uses the trick to contact a friend in a British prison during the Revolution. In the course of the
scene, the claim is made that the Revolution is only
another Popish plot against King George.[29]   Ingraham's
Captain Kyd is a long narrative set both in Ireland and
in the colonies. The villain, known as Father Nanfan,
tries in the usual manner to seduce the heroine through
use of the confessional. He is later revealed to be
a pirate.[30]

The treatment of the Church in the various colonies

---

[27]St. George Tucker, Hansford: A Tale of Bacon's
Rebellion (Richmond: George M. West, 1857), p. 93.

[28]Tucker, Hansford, pp. 355-356.

[29]Emerson Bennett, Rosalie Dupont; or, Treason in the
Camp. A Story of the Revolution (Cincinnati: U. P. James,
cop. 1853), p. 11.

[30]Joseph Holt Ingraham, Captain Kyd; or, The Wizard
of the Sea (New York: Harper and Brothers, 1839), pp. 111-
113.

is almost a reversal of the pattern in Europe; the French
colonial Church is the most benevolent, and the English
the most Gothic. This reversal is caused by the differing
political situation in the colonies; neither French nor
Spanish possessions stood very strongly in the way of
the American destiny, and so never acquired the aspect of
menace in the imagination of these authors. In England,
on the other hand, Catholic influence was associated with
the attempts to revoke Colonial charters in the Seventeenth Century; the political image of the Church therefore appears. Even so, the menace is far milder than in
the European version of the Gothic Church.

The Church in the United States

Excluding the Irish characters, the Church in the
United States is not a major concern in the fiction of
the sample. Priests, for example, are mainly shown in
brief roles, and do not affect the movement of the plot.
One appears simply to administer the sacraments to a dying
Catholic.[31] An ex-priest and his wife (he a professor at
Williams College) live and die peacefully; the wife is
buried as a Catholic.[32] In another novel, a Father
Angelo, a mysterious hermit (not clearly identified as

---

[31]Eliza Henderson Otis, The Barclays of Boston (Boston: Ticknor, Reed, and Fields, 1854), p. 342.

[32]Gerrit van Husen Forbes, Green Mountain Annals (New
York: Burnett and Smith, 1832), pp. 120-131.

a Catholic priest), is a respected and saintly man.[33]
Even in connection with Irish parishioners, few priests
are brought in. One priest is shown reading letters for
his illiterate people, and questioning them on their
employers' religious attitudes, thus keeping a measure of
control over them.[34] Other references to priests are
vague and do not define the type further.

The figure of the nun is a bit exotic, but distinctly
moderate. J. H. Ingraham observed Catholic institutions
in Louisiana and Mississippi and found nothing ominous.
He described the convent schools as good, and discovered
no proselytizing of non-Catholic girls; he thought the
prospects for lasting conversions among the people of
the South to be poor.[35] He thought the convents were
romantic, though full of "fair prisoners."[36] Sisters seem
to have been rare sights, according to Cooper: "In 1803,
a nun and a nunnery would be almost as great curiosities,
in America, as a rhinoceros, though the country has since
undergone some changes in this respect." Seeing a figure

---

[33]Caroline Lee Hentz, The Lost Daughter, and Other
Stories of the Heart (Philadelphia: T. B. Peterson,
cop. 1857), pp. 1-54.

[34]Louisa Caroline Tuthill, The Belle, The Blue, and
The Bigot; or, Three Fields for Woman's Influence (Providence: Samuel C. Blodget, 1844), pp. 261-262.

[35]Joseph Holt Ingraham, The South-West. By A Yankee
(New York: Harper and Brothers, 1835), I, 194; I, 251.

[36]Ingraham, South-West, I, 250.

of a nun in a wax museum, his New Yorkers are bewildered:

> "It isn't _Lady_ Washington, is it?"
> "It looks more like a clergyman's wife. . . ."
> "A nun! . . . Isn't that the sort of woman that
> shuts herself up in a house, and promises never
> to get married?"[37]

There is a scene of a girl entering a convent in the Mid-
west, which gives her erstwhile lover the conventional
thrill of fear.[38]

The only striking nun is a strange figure indeed;
Mrs. Courtlandt, Sister of Mercy and Superior of a convent
school in western Virginia. She wears a man's cutaway
coat, a short skirt, and boots; her school seems socially
liberal (the girls dance the minuet); and she has a vein
of rough humor.[39] Hunter John Myers, a character modelled
on Natty Bumppo, distrusts her because she once "spelled"
his rifle. She charged it with a Leyden jar for a joke;
and though Myers claims that she "doesn't stand well in
these parts," she seems to stand well enough with the
author.[40] She is a bluff, original character, who surely
helps to banish the Gothic vision of the Church.

A few stories take up immigrant characters who happen

---

[37]Cooper, _Afloat_ and _Ashore_, III, 148-149.

[38]Martha Allen, _Day-Dreams_ (Philadelphia: Lippincott,
Grambe and Co., 1854), pp. 188-194.

[39]John Esten Cooke, _Leather Stocking and Silk_; _or_,
Hunter John Myers and His Times (New York: Harper and
Brothers, 1854), pp. 27, 40.

[40]Cooke, _Leather Stocking_, pp. 166-167.

to be Catholics. In all of these stories the sympathy
of the author lies with the immigrant, and their religion does not operate against them.[41] A scattered few
stories mention Catholics in other contexts, but none of
them is important, and none is hostile or Gothic in its
implications.[42]

As for the intellectual face of the Church, John
Delavan Bryant's Pauline Seward is the only full-length
treatment of a Catholic subject in the setting of the
contemporary United States, and it is a novel of conversion.[43] The book is devoted to the process of converting
the entire Seward family from Presbyterianism to Catholicism. Although it does contain an interesting exchange
of views among Protestants on the Nativist riots in Philadelphia in 1844, there is very little about the immigrant

---

[41]Lydia Maria Child, Letters From New York. Second
Series (New York: C. S. Francis and Co., 1845), p. 150ff.;
Frederick William Thomas, Sketches of Character, and Tales
Founded on Fact (Louisville: Chronicle of Western Litera-
ture and Art, 1849), p. 96; Sara Jane Lippincott, Green-
wood Leaves: A Collection of Sketches and Letters (Boston:
Ticknor, Reed, and Fields, 1850), p. 153ff.

[42]David Brown, The Planter; or, Thirteen Years in the
South (Philadelphia: H. Hooker, 1853), p. 70; Lippincott,
Greenwood Leaves. Second Series (Boston: Ticknor, Reed,
and Fields, 1852), p. 111; Frederick Swartwout Cozzens,
The Sparrowgrass Papers; or, Living in the Country (New
York: Derby and Jackson, 1856), p. 145.

[43]John Delavan Bryant, Pauline Seward: A Tale of Real
Life (Baltimore: John Murphy; Pittsburg: George Quigley;
Dublin: R. Grace and Sons, 1847). The material on Phila-
delphia is Vol. I, pp. 190ff.

in the book. It is a standard sort of narrative, working
its way through all of the historical arguments for the
Roman Catholic Church as the true Church which Christ
founded, in a series of discussions between Pauline and
her mentors. Bryant himself was a convert, and makes
little effort to disguise the didacticism of the work.
This kind of book is scarcely objective about religious
matters, and it is careful not to contaminate the Church
with the image of the immigrant. Orestes Brownson re-
viewed the book, and was harsh about both it and its type;
the problem being that these novels are not needed by
the converted, and generally bore the unconverted to
tears.[44]

Generally speaking, then, the Catholic characters in
the novels set in the United States are treated moderately
and realistically, though they are not very common, and
have small parts to play. Some of the Gothic elements are
present in embryo, but there do not seem to be pressures
to exploit them in this context. A suggestion of the
light approach to the Gothic ideas is in a sketch by Eliza
Leslie. The ladies of a literary club gather for the
reading of a novel "descriptive of murderous noblemen,

[44]Brownson's Quarterly Review (New Series), I (1847),
p. 216, a review of four books, including Bryant's. In
the same volume, p. 117, is a review of seven Catholic
novels, in the same vein.

sentimental cottagers, diabolical monks, and graceful robbers. . . . the monk being incog. all through."[45]

The Irish and the Church

The striking thing about the Irish characters in these books is the minor role that religious interest and religious practice have in their parts. References which unambiguously identify Irish characters as either Catholic or Protestant are confined to fewer than twenty books. It would seem safe to say that Irish are expected to be Catholics, in the general pattern of the image. At least, the great majority of the Irish are Catholics, when the question arises; but it does not arise often. Even when religion appears as an Irish trait, there is little of the powerful or political side of the Church in it.

In an indirect way, Irish may be identified as Catholics by their speech. Swearing by saints or relics is the most frequent of these signs.[46] This habit may of

---

[45]Eliza Leslie, Pencil Sketches; or, Outlines of Character and Manners. Second Series (Philadelphia: Carey, Lea and Blanchard, 1835), pp. 91-92.

[46]Swearing by St. Patrick:
Joseph Holt Ingraham, The South-West. By a Yankee (New York: Harper and Brothers, 1835), II, 21; Charles Sealsfield (Karl Anton Postl), Life in the New World; or, Sketches of American Society (New York: J. Winchester, New World Press, cop. 1844), p. 76.
Swearing by Jesus:
Joseph B. Cobb, Mississippi Scenes; or, Sketches of Southern and Western Life and Adventure (Philadelphia: A. Hart, 1851), p. 142; Asa Greene, The Perils of Pearl Street;

course be more a cultural pattern than a sign of personal commitment or devotion to the saint; but the habit is a Catholic one, not a Protestant one. Other religious patterns serving to distinguish Catholics from Protestants among the Irish in the sample are devotion to the saints,[47] beliefs in such things as Purgatory and prayers for the dead,[48] and practices like confession,

---

Including a Taste of the Dangers of Wall Street (New York: Betts and Anstice, and Peter Hill, 1834), p. 127.
By the true cross:
Paul Jones: A Tale of the Sea (Philadelphia: A. J. Rockefellar, 1843), p. 34.
By saints in general:
Justin Jones, Mad Jack and Gentleman Jack; or, The Last Cruise of Old Ironsides Around the World (Boston: Star Spangled Banner Office, 1850), p. 59; Elhanan Winchester Reynolds, Records of the Bubbleton Parish (Boston: A. Tompkins and B. B. Mussey and Co., 1854), p. 136.

[47]Devotion to St. Patrick is noted in:
Francis Colburn Adams, Our World; or, The Slaveholder's Daughter (New York and Auburn: Miller, Orton, and Mulligan, 1855), p. 574; The Brigantine; or, Admiral Lowe (New York: Crowen and Decker, 1839), p. 47.
Herman Melville, Typee; A Peep at Polynesian Life (New York: Wiley and Putnam; London: John Murray, 1846), p. 60, refers to the legend of St. Patrick expelling the snakes from Ireland.
Devotion to Mary is mentioned only in Martha Russell, Leaves From the Tree Igdrasyl (Boston: John P. Jewett; Cleveland: Jewett, Proctor, and Worthington; New York: Sheldon, Lamport, and Blakeman, 1854), p. 70.

[48]Purgatory: Russell, Leaves from Igdrasyl, p. 169.
Praying for the dead: M. M. Ballou, Roderic the Rover; or, The Spirit of the Wave (Boston: F. Gleason, 1849), p. 26.
Difficulty of salvation for Protestants: Which: The Right, or the Left? (New York: Garrett and Co., 1855), p. 129.

attending Mass, and making the sign of the cross.[49]
Very little in the way of implication is made of these
references, however distinctive they may be. The tone
is generally neutral; Catholic elements are simply part
of the national identity.

The small number of Irish in the sample who are
not Catholic should be noted. Britannia O'Riley, in
Mrs. Southworth's The Mother-in-Law, is apparently
Episcopalian, an affiliation in keeping with her aristocratic connections in Ireland.[50] Dr. McBrain, in
Cooper's The Ways of the Hour, had an Irish grandfather
(possibly from Ulster), and is certainly not a Catholic.[51]
Another family descended from Irish of Revolutionary times
is Protestant in the present generation.[52] A character
with the fanciful name of McBowline harasses the narrator

---

[49]Confession: twice in Sara Payson Parton, Fresh
Leaves. By Fanny Fern (New York: Mason Brothers, 1857),
pp. 164, 264; also in Catherine Maria Sedgwick, Clarence;
or, A Tale of Our Times (Philadelphia: Carey and Lea,
1830), I, 71.
Mass and Lent: Sara Josepha Hale, "Boarding Out." A Tale
of Domestic Life (New York: Harper and Brothers, 1846),
p. 63.
Sign of the Cross: Russell, Leaves from Igdrasyl, p. 70.

[50]Emma Dorothy Eliza Nevitt Southworth, The Mother-
in-Law: A Tale of Domestic Life (Philadelphia: T. B.
Peterson and Brothers, cop. 1860).

[51]James Fenimore Cooper, The Ways of the Hour (New
York: George P. Putnam, 1850), p. 56.

[52]Mary Virginia Terhune, Nemesis (New York: Derby
and Jackson, 1860), pp. 19-28.

of My Uncle Hobson and I, stealing his wallet while both
are attending a Millerite revival--surely no place for
a Catholic.[53]   In two books, Irish children are taught in
Protestant Sunday schools; in another, an Irish maid is
converted by her employer's kindness.[54]

If few Irish, and those mostly of a special kind,
are Protestant, even fewer Irish show any signs of dis-
affection from Catholicism.   There are no real rebels.
One character refers to the sad state of "praste-ridden"
Ireland, and another praises the Irishmen who have fought
"oppression" at home and in exile.[55]   Presumably the
oppression might include Church as well as State, though
that is not made explicit.

Rather, the Irish were more likely to be loyal to
their religion in the controversies of the day.   The dangerous possibilities in this loyalty are suggested in
Judson's The Volunteer, which refers to a company of Irish
and other Catholics who have deserted to Santa Anna in

---

[53]Pascal Jones, My Uncle Hobson and I; or, Slashes at
Life with a Free Broad-Axe (New York: D. Appleton and Co.;
Philadelphia: Geo. S. Appleton, 1845), pp. 126-148.

[54]Sunday school incidents in: Isabel; or, Trials of
the Heart (New York: Harper and Brothers, 1845), p. 127;
Parton, Fresh Leaves, p. 327.
The conversion of the maid: Tuthill, The Belle, The Blue,
and The Bigot, p. 264.

[55]Vidi (pseud.), Mr. Frank, The Underground Mail-
Agent (Philadelphia: Lippincott, Grambo and Co., 1853),
p. 115; Edmund Farrenc, Carlotina and the Sanfedisti,
p. 390.

the Mexican War.[56] But the war was distant, and other
references to Irish defenses of the Church are mild.
Catholic loyalty does not seem in them to demand disloyalty to America. An Irishman can defend the Pope
against a hostile preacher; he can exaggerate the Pope's
powers, and come to blows with the crowd, without evoking
much more than benevolent amusement from the author.[57]
In another case, a Protestant attacks the European Sunday:
"You Catholics won't be allowed to desecrate the Sabbath
in this way much longer."[58] The Catholic Irish apple-
seller replies sharply, and the author seems to side with
her.

Nor do the Irishman's priests present much of a
threat. There are not many of them, and they are mildly
treated. The priest who reared and educated Rose Brady
is a good and sensible man, who exerted no unhealthy power
over her.[59] Another priest is a figure in a farce. "Jim
Soolivan" is thought dead; his wife at once remarries
(with a fee to the priest). When Jim returns, the priest

---

[56]Edward Zane Carroll Judson, The Volunteer; or, The
Maid of Monterrey. By Ned Buntline (Boston: Published by
F. Gleason, The Flag of Our Union Office, 1847), p. 57.

[57]Mortimer Neal Thomson, Doesticks' Letters: And What
He Says (Philadelphia: T. B. Peterson and Brothers,
cop. 1855), p. 109.

[58]Child, Letters From New York, p. 166.

[59]Charlotte Ann Jerauld, "Rose Brady," Poetry and
Prose (Boston: A. Tompkins, 1850), pp. 398-416.

is called to exorcise the "ghost," a rite for which he charges the widow twelve pounds. When Jim proves to be alive, the priest marries him to his wife again, for another fee.[60] Another comic priest is Father O'Callaghan, who advised a parishioner that she could drink in "self-defense."[61] Apart from a hint of greed, which is shared by the Mexican priests who protect Aunt Beck because of her generosity to the Church,[62] these men are simply comic. The most interesting of the priests who relate to Irish does exert moral authority. He is the priest in The Belle, The Blue, and The Bigot who questions the servant girls about their employers' religious attitudes. He has been a general guide to them, reading their letters from home to them and writing letters for them, and he tries to supervise their religious lives. The author refers to him as a "sensible man," who "exerted his influence over his people more for their temporal than their spiritual good."[63] He does seem intent on preventing assimilation, and on preserving national (and therefore religious) identity.

---

[60]"Jim Soolivan," Humorist Tales, pp. 11-18.

[61]Lucius Manlius Sargent, The Stage-Coach. Founded on Fact (Boston: Whipple and Damrell; New York: Scofield and Voorhies, 1838), pp. 199-210.

[62]Charles Wilkins Webber, Tales of the Southern Border (Philadelphia: Lippincott, Grambo and Co., 1853), pp. 128-129.

[63]Tuthill, The Belle, pp. 258-259.

There is really nothing Gothic about any of these priests, except possibly the Mexicans; there is also very little spiritual about them. Most interesting is their rarity. Only these four Irish priests appear. No Irish character is cast as a monk or nun; no Irishman is a bishop. Irish are excluded from these dangerous and enticing roles. The absence of bishops is especially curious; figures for this can be found. A substantial number of American bishops in 1850 were born in Ireland or had immigrant parents, including most of the bishops of the North and East; and among the group was the most vocal and controversial figure in the American Catholic Church, Archbishop John Hughes of New York.[64]

The Irish characters with large roles, all of whom have been treated in earlier chapters, are nearly all Catholic. When the characters are viewed affectionately, their Catholicism is also accepted kindly. Such is the case with Barney Pike, the comic servant of Wyoming. His rosary and crucifix stir up comic alarm in the maid; later his reverence for priests leads him to let Father Janaway

---

[64]In 1850, there were thirty-two bishops in the United States. Eleven of them were of Irish descent; seven were born in Ireland. The Irish bishops included those of New York, Philadelphia, Boston, Pittsburgh, Albany, Hartford, and Wheeling. Only Buffalo and Baltimore had non-Irish bishops in the Northeastern area. Material from The Catholic Encyclopedia (New York, 1907-1912), and The Official Catholic Directory (New York, annual).

escape.[65] Joe Beck, of _Wild_ _Western_ _Scenes,_ in his comic

fear of death, prays in Latin (thought by a Texan to be

"purgatory language") and begs for a priest.[66] In both

cases, Catholic elements are made the object of laughter,

but there is no real criticism. The O'Morra family, in

Rosemary, is proudly Catholic, though little is done with

actual religious practice.[67]

The attitude does not change much even in regard to

the Irish characters who show criminal traits. Conolly

committed perjury partly because of his pique at the doc-

tor who did not call a priest for a dying Catholic; his

religion thus failed to keep him honest, and helped cause

his crime. The blame, however, is laid on his childish-

ness.[68] Kate O'Donnell, in _Estelle_ _Grant,_ refers to her

fear of the priest, but her life is violent; religion

cannot be held responsible for it, however. She is

clearly acting against her training.[69] Aunt Beck, who is

---

[65]Caleb Wright, _Wyoming:_ _A_ _Tale_ (New York: Harper and Brothers, 1845), pp. 15, 88.

[66]John Beauchamp Jones, _Wild_ _Western_ _Scenes:_ _A_ _Narra-_ _tive_ _of_ _Adventures_ _in_ _the_ _Western_ _Wilderness,_ _Forty_ _Years_ _Ago_ (Philadelphia: E. Ferrett and Co., 1845), pp. 99, 244.

[67]Jedediah Vincent Huntington, _Rosemary;_ _or,_ _Life_ _and_ _Death_ (New York, Boston and Montreal: D. and J. Sadlier and Co., 1860).

[68]Catherine Maria Sedgwick, _Clarence;_ _or,_ _A_ _Tale_ _of_ _Our_ _Times_ (Philadelphia: Carey and Lea, 1830), I, 71.

[69]_Estelle_ _Grant;_ _or,_ _The_ _Lost_ _Wife_ (New York: Garrett and Co., cop. 1855).

a professional smuggler and a hard case generally--she murdered her husband--remains within the Church. She has made gestures of repentance, by going on pilgrimage and by generous donations.[70] There is a suggestion in this pattern of connivance on the part of the Church; Aunt Beck is treated more leniently because of her money. The author's attitude seems neither shocked nor surprised; smuggling has never been regarded as the worst of crimes. Even in the case of the much reviled Finnegan, religion is lightly treated. His identity as a Catholic is coarsely put; his mouth, says the author, was designed for eating codfish on Fridays.[71] But though Finnegan steals, takes bribes, and drinks to excess, little more is said about his church. His last request for the priest, when he is about to be hanged, is rejected by the native gang; and the situation would seem to evoke a certain amount of sympathy for him.

The same complex of ideas is used in defining Irish Catholicism as in defining Catholicism in general; it is composed of those items which had long been distinctive and controversial between Catholics and Protestants. Confession and the anointing at death, both sacraments in

---

[70]Webber, Tales of Southern Border, pp. 128-129, 132.

[71]George Thompson, The Brazen Star; or, The Adventures of a New-York M.P. (New York: George W. Hill, 1853), pp. 22-24.

Catholic teaching and not in Protestant, are two of these
items. Papal supremacy, the use of the rosary, devotion
to the saints, abstinence from meat, and belief in purgatory are others. One supposes that these would immediately spring to mind in describing a Catholic character,
and would be used in the book to illustrate Catholic religious behavior. This constitutes a kind of Catholic
convention, a concept divorced from observation. That
Catholics always wound up arguing these points with Protestants does not imply that they occupied the major place
in the day to day lives of the people. The central religious act of the Catholics of the time, including the
Irish, would presumably have been the Mass, and the most
important sacrament (after baptism) would have been holy
communion. These are scarcely mentioned at all; most of
the masses brought in are masses for funerals or for the
dead, and therefore touch on peculiar Catholic beliefs
about purgatory. Presumably the liturgy of the mass and
of communion are less controversial because there are
Protestant parallels.

It is clear at any rate that the convention of Irish
Catholic life, though it remains limited to traditionally
unique Catholic elements, includes nothing at all resembling the Gothic aspect of the European Church. We have
seen that the Gothic, political, authoritarian Church has

little attention given in any work set in the United
States, though it is perennially useful in France and
Italy. This seems to imply for the church at large that
Catholicism is imaginatively evil, a symbol of the old
and repressive Europe; but that the image cannot be trans-
planted. There are no symbols in America that will bear
it. The Irish share in the tolerant view of the Church
that follows from this; they are exempt further by their
evident incapacity for holding positions of authority.
In the face of the fact that Irish had high positions in
the Church in America, the image excludes them from the
hierarchy.

VI. CONVENTION AND ASSIMILATION

The material presented in the preceding chapters resists easy generalizations and does not permit the construction of a single consistent image of the Irish. There is rather a collection of reactions by American writers to the presence of the Irish. The quality and direction of the reaction depends in each case on the situation in which the Irish character appears. Ultimately each variety of the Irish character derives from the total context of tension or peaceful adjustment which his presence produces.

If we use the whole array of Irish character types as the background for the question, "Can America accept and assimilate the Irish?," the answer as provided by American fiction seems to be affirmative. In spite of isolated examples of Irish characters constructed to cast doubt on the possibility of their Americanization, the general tenor of these examples is positive. When the attention of the book is on the Irish as a problem-- generally in connection with slavery or Nativist feeling-- rhetoric is likely to dominate. In the more numerous cases in which the Irish characters occur naturally, most of the Irish traits seem easily compatible with American institutions.

The simple fact is that the Irish character in this period of American fiction is not important in the novels in which it appears. Except for a few cases such as those noted above, Irish are at the periphery of the events in the stories, and their fate is not a matter of concern. The Irishman is simply ineligible to be the hero of a novel. He is barred by class from the marriage that crowns the life of the hero of a romantic narrative, and from the full glory of the successful adventure. It is a rare Irish character who has a significant action to perform in a plot, and generally this character is a servant.

Despite the large number of books in which the Irish appear, the total effect is minor. This fact has significance for the problem of assimilation in two ways. First, in spite of the critical problems raised in religion, politics, and society by the influx of immigrants, the American mind as manifested by the books in the sample did not regard the Irishman as a genuinely serious threat. Doesticks' Letters, which turns all Irish appearances, riotous or violent, into humorous anecdotes, is perhaps the clearest illustration of this.[1] Second, the presented

---

[1]Mortimer Neal Thomson, Doesticks' Letters: And What He Says (Philadelphia: T. B. Peterson and Brothers, cop. 1855).

Irish character falls into conventional habits and behavior long familiar in literature, holding no terrors at
all; the authors seem to have picked up the easy keys to
characterizing the Irish, without reference to the real-
ities around them. Nothing could be more tame and comfortable than the literary Irishman.

To speak of the function of convention as a factor
favorable to assimilation, and to do so with reasonable
assurance, requires a definition of the content of the
Irish type. The preceding chapters have discussed specific aspects of the character as they appear under a
variety of settings and in a variety of plots. Generalizations in terms of types only blur the outlines without
defining a broader type. Certain consistent qualities
can be found in the broad range of the characters, however. The following discussion will center on three of
those aspects of the Irish character; passivity, comic
optimism, and Catholicism. Each of these, as will appear,
can be seen first of all as an aid to assimilation of
the image, and secondly as an element of conventionality,
differing in greater or lesser degree from actuality.

Docility and Acceptance of Dependent Status

Irish characters in the fiction are virtually devoid
of aggressiveness and competitiveness. They show no
desire for wealth, they do not seek office or power

(though they may have strong party feeling), and the men do not pursue American women. This sort of passivity seems to imply deficient American values, since ambition and the drive for status are acceptable in the native hero. The suggestion of passive acceptance is demeaning to the Irish character also in assuming that he is likely to be content in whatever place society is willing to offer. Since that place is uniformly very low, the Irish character is expected to be satisfied with the crumbs from the American table.

The important aspect of this quality, however, is the reassurance it offers the American audience. A character so willing to accept inferior status is no threat to the structure of the society it enters. Politically passive, economically inert, and in no way a sexual rival to the native, the Irishman of fiction is harmless. As a symbol, the Irish pattern of marrying Irish is the most important guarantee of his low status and of his harmlessness. The stock Negro character in the period could suggest primitive sexuality; the Irishman could not. Both men and women among the Irish are remarkably free of passion.

This lack of sexuality--or rather, the nearly absolute rule that Irish marry only Irish--makes the fictional Irishman easier to accept. A powerful source of hostility is diverted. There is in this too an implication of childishness, of the lack of full adult needs and choices. The very rare selection of an Irish wife by an American character does not alter the pattern, because this is the more acceptable side of the marriage across national lines, and because these marriages follow class lines.[2]

Oscar Handlin has presented some statistics on marriages in Boston in the years 1860 to 1863, indicating the place of nativity of brides and grooms.[3] According

---

[2]Marriages of this kind occur in William Leete Stone, Ups and Downs in the Life of a Distressed Gentleman (New York: Leavitt, Lord and Co.; Boston: Crocker and Brewster, 1836); Charlotte Ann Jerauld, "The Irish Daughter-in-Law," Poetry and Prose (Boston: A. Tompkins, 1850); and Emma Dorothy Eliza Nevitte Southworth, The Mother-in-Law: A Tale of Domestic Life (Philadelphia: T. B. Peterson and Brothers, cop. 1860) (first published 1851).

[3]Oscar Handlin, Boston's Immigrants: A Study in Acculturation, rev. and enl. ed. (Cambridge: Harvard University Press, 1959), Table XXVII, p. 259. The table lists 2,378 grooms born in Ireland, 2,596 brides born in Ireland, and 1,997 marriages in which both parties were born in Ireland.

Though the book deals only with Boston, much use must be made of it; it is unique in the possession of firm generalizations based on careful quantification.

Other general works on the Irish, especially Carl Wittke, The Irish in America (Baton Rouge: Louisiana State University Press, 1956), are helpful for general atmosphere, but tend to be anecdotal, and do not provide a ground for generalizations. Handlin's The Uprooted (Boston: Little, Brown and Co., 1952) is an excellent introduction to the experience of the immigrant, done from their own records. Cecil Woodham-Smith, The Great Hunger (New York: Harper and Row, 1962), is the best account of the famine, and contains a great deal about the conditions of emigration, though very little about the American experiences.

to these figures, 84 per cent of men born in Ireland married brides born in Ireland, and 77 per cent of brides born in Ireland married grooms born in Ireland.[4] The percentage of national marriages is probably higher still, since children of Irish parents might be listed with Boston or other United States nativity. The figures as they appear, however, show a very strong tendency to marry within the group; they also show the slightly greater freedom of Irish women to marry American men which is suggested by the fiction. The possible variables in these statistics make a firm deduction impossible. It would seem safe to say that fiction in this instance follows actuality, though the fictional rule is more rigid than the actuality seems to have been.

Acceptance of low economic status is another aspect of the fictional character on which Handlin's statistics

[4]By comparison, from the same table, only 58% of grooms born in Germany married brides born in Germany, though 86% of brides born in Germany married grooms born in Germany. For Great Britain the figures are 20% of British born grooms marrying British brides, 28% of British brides marrying British grooms. Handlin, Boston's Immigrants, Table XXVII, p. 259.

cast light.[5] Over three-fourths of the laborers in Boston
in 1850 were Irish, as were two-thirds of the domestic
servants. These are the most common occupations for fictional Irish, of course, and are thoroughly rooted in
the British convention. Together they accounted for
63 per cent of all the Irish working in Boston. Once
again the convention and the actual conditions run in
similar patterns.

There are a few surprises in the listing, however.
The third largest group of Irish were listed as tailors;
the 1,045 in that category were two-thirds of the tailors
in Boston, and accounted for 7 per cent of all Irish workers. One-third of the smiths, and about the same proportion of shoemakers and leatherworkers, were Irish, and so
were a significant number of masons. None of these trades

---

[5]Handlin, Boston's Immigrants, Table XIII, pp. 248-
249. This table (derived with ingenious labor from the
Census data of 1850) shows the number of Irish in various
trades. Some of the more common Irish jobs:

Occupation	Total workers in occupation	Irish workers
Laborers	8,552	7,007
Domestic Servants	3,249	2,292
Tailors	1,547	1,045
Shoemakers	570	206
Masons	764	203
Carpenters	2,053	356
Smiths	877	307
Pedlers, traders	1,183	211

The total number of persons in the work force was 43,567;
total of Irish in the work force, 14,595.

have entered into the literary image of the Irish, who
never became characterized as skilled labor. Any one of
those trades would seem to fit the image of the later
Italian immigrant, for instance. Even allowing for the
fact that many of the Irish tailors or shoemakers were
probably in the new factories, which did not teach or
require a craftsman's skill, the complete exclusion of
the Irish character from this kind of occupation seems
to indicate that convention is at work.

Here again is possible evidence of the convention
steering attention away from the competitive threat of
the Irishman. If the image is confined to manual labor
and domestic service, both areas which natives would be
glad to assign to the newcomers, there is no threat to
displace American workers or to disrupt the patterns of
opportunity.

Religious Pessimism or Comic Optimism

Analyzing the discordant relations between the
natives and the Irish, Handlin describes the conflict
between the pessimism and supernaturalism of the immigrants and the "rationalism and . . . all-pervading optimism" of the Bostonians.

> [At home] the Irish had found little in
> life that was not dark and nothing that was
> hopeful. Their utter helplessness before the

most elemental forces fostered an immense sad-
ness, a deep-rooted pessimism about the world
and man's role in it. . . .[6]

The journey to America, with the poverty and over-

crowded slums they found, did nothing to change their

views. Nor did their religion, which put its major

emphasis on salvation and the afterlife, and scorned the

world and its promises of progress. In regard to the

revolutions of 1848, for instance, which were at first

enthusiastically hailed by the Irish, the official Church

eventually sided with conservatism and stifled democratic

sentiments.[7]

The Irish in fiction, on the contrary. are joyful,

comic, indefeasible in their good humor, under any kind of

difficulty, whether in war or the courts of law. The con-

ventional Irishman imitates Teague O'Regan in his blithe

confidence in his own ability to fill any role. The sober

and respectable Irish in the books, such as the O'Morra

family in Rosemary, share fully the American values of

hard work, security, and the respect of their neighbors.

Where the politics of Irish characters are known, they are

not in the least conservative, and religion (except as

a reaction against Nativism) seldom appears to enter into

politics, at least at this period.

---

[6]Handlin, Boston's Immigrants, pp. 124-125.

[7]Handlin, Boston's Immigrants, pp. 138-141.

The literary Irishman is here in full conflict with the state of affairs which Handlin has described. The conventional ebullience of the Irish character dominates the fictional view. Like passivity, this persistent good humor is a limiting trait, implying a kind of childishness. It also implies harmlessness, of course. Handlin has described a real conflict of outlook between Irish and Americans, which could and did affect public feelings on a variety of issues. The practically complete exclusion of this version of the Irish mind from the fiction, whatever its causes, removes this source of conflict. The comic, optimistic Irishman is Americanized, in a way. Conventional expectations make the comic Irishman acceptable; but it would seem that the authors of the books are consciously or unconsciously suppressing their awareness of the actual, contentious Irishman, or so unreal a convention would fade.

"Native" Irish and Ulster Scots

There were during this period--and still are--three racial and religious strains in the population of Ireland. The native Irish, almost exclusively Catholic, were the large majority. Anglo-Irish, generally belonging to the Church of Ireland, were the descendants of English landlords and government officials. The Ulster Scots, also called Scotch-Irish, descended from colonists planted in

Ireland during the seventeenth century, were Presbyterian.

All of these might identify themselves as Irish, all would appear in immigration figures as coming from Ireland, and presumably some of each group did in fact emigrate. It is almost impossible to distinguish the groups in retrospect, especially since historians among the Irish are likely to claim Irish surnames for whichever group they favor. Anglo-Irish might be the least likely to emigrate, because of their higher status in Ireland. Ulster Scots seem to have predominated in the immigration before 1800; when Brackenridge noted that the West was "half Ireland," he clearly distinguished them from the "aboriginal" Irish.[8] The later immigration, especially the great flood in the great famine, was largely Catholic. It seems that some proportion of this later group were Ulster Scots, but it is impossible to tell how many. Marcus Hansen points to a rather large movement of Protestant Irish around 1830.[9]

---

[8]Hugh Henry Brackenridge, Modern Chivalry, ed. Claude M. Newlin (New York: American Book Co., 1937), p. 405. First pub. 1792-1815. Robert E. Blanc, James McHenry, Playwright and Novelist (Philadelphia: University of Pennsylvania, 1939), p. 49, indicates that Ulster characters in McHenry's work speak in an accent resembling Scottish.

[9]Marcus W. Hansen, The Atlantic Migration: 1607-1860 (Cambridge: Harvard University Press, 1940), p. 134: ". . . the government agent at Quebec estimating that five-sixths of the incoming passengers were from Ulster. The usual comment in describing the departure of a vessel, that two-thirds of those on board were Protestants, affords additional evidence."

The point of this is that there were at least a substantial number of people in the United States during
the period who were either Protestant Irish immigrants
or the descendants of Protestant Irish; specifically,
Presbyterian Ulstermen. If, however, the sample of fiction is taken as a measure, there were practically no
Irish at all except the Catholics. Anglo-Irish, represented by military officers and Britannia O'Riley, are
more frequent than Ulster Scots.[10] Dr. McBrain, in
Cooper's Ways of the Hour, admits to an Irish grandfather,
presumably an Ulsterman;[11] but even in the West and South-
west there are no other characters so identified. All
indications of speech, religion, and national traits are
overwhelmingly those of the Catholic Irish.

This suggests that the authors in the sample followed
Brackenridge's lead in using the "aboriginal" Irishman
as the standard version of the character, regardless of
the actual nature of the Irish population. Their reasons
may have been similar to his: that the Catholic Irish
character was well established and easy to use, and readily recognized by the audience. The effect of this choice
is to make the fictional image Irishman practically purely
that of a Catholic Irishman.

---

[10]Southworth, The Mother-in-Law.

[11]James Fenimore Cooper, The Ways of The Hour. A Tale
(New York: George P. Putnam, 1850), p. 56.

This would seem at first glance to make assimilation
more difficult, not less, as has been apparently true
in the traits previously discussed. Catholicism, however,
has always been part of the Irish image in British convention, and little serious conflict came out of it. As we
have seen in the fictional treatments of the Catholic
Church, the vicious aspects of Catholic power are seen in
French or Italian contexts, and Irish are treated very
kindly. Their qualities of passivity and easy acceptance
of American values--fictionally speaking--remove the Irish
Catholic from the menace of the Gothic Church. Irish
Catholics were not identified with the power of the hierarchy, even though most American bishops were Irish, and
they were not tainted with the monarchist politics of
Rome. The Irishman, because he is portrayed as a comic,
childish, blundering, conventional Catholic "aboriginal,"
will never force his religion or his will on other Americans. Not even Finnegan is accused of royal or Papal
ambitions.

Conclusion

These aspects of the Irish image in literature,
sometimes reasonably close to actuality and sometimes
far removed, have been advanced in order to demonstrate
the persistence of the Irish convention and to indicate
the ways in which the convention might ease the

intellectual acceptance of the Irishman in American life.
By and large the Irish character in literature is perfectly harmless and thoroughly at home. Actual immigrants
must have been far more diverse, much more troublesome,
much more disturbing than these fictional shadows; it is
a matter for regret that no one cared enough or saw enough
to make them the subject of serious attention. Still,
the very careless, easygoing use of false but friendly
stereotypes in fiction must have helped to ease the en-
trance of the real Irish into American life.

BIBLIOGRAPHY

I. American Fiction 1830-1860

The titles in this listing comprise the sample of fiction from which the material for this study is drawn. All titles are in the holdings of the Library of the University of Pennsylvania. With few exceptions, all are in Lyle H. Wright's lists of American fiction, and the number in that list appears after each entry. W I refers to Lyle H. Wright, American Fiction: 1774-1850; W II refers to Wright, American Fiction: 1851-1875.

Books cited in the text are marked with an asterisk.

[Abbott, Anne Wales, ed.] Autumn Leaves. Original Pieces in Prose and Verse. Cambridge: John Bartlett, 1853.
     W II 1.

* [Adams, Francis Colburn.] Our World; or, The Slave-holder's Daughter. New York and Auburn: Miller, Orton and Mulligan, 1855.
     W II 13.

* [Adams, William Taylor.] In Doors and Out; or, Views from the Chimney Corner. By Oliver Optic. Boston: Brown, Bazin and Co., 1855.
     W II 26.

Alden, Joseph. The Old Revolutionary Soldier. New York: Gates and Stedman, 1848.
     W I 11.

* Allen, Martha. Day-Dreams: with Additions. 2d. ed. Philadelphia: Lippincott, Grambo and Co., 1854.
     W II 56.

Ambrose and Eleanor; or, The Disinherited Pair. A Tale of the Revolution. By an Officer. New York: Joseph A. Clussman, 1834.
     W I 19.

167

Arthur, Timothy Shay.   The Beautiful Widow. . . .
      Philadelphia: Carey and Hart, 1847.
            W I 56.

_____. The Debtor's Daughter; or, Life and its
Changes. Philadelphia: T. B. Peterson [cop. 1850].
            W I 68.

_____. Finger Posts on the Way of Life.
Boston: L. P. Crown and Co.; Philadelphia: J. W.
Bradley, 1853.
            W II 91.

_____. Golden Grains from Life's Harvest
Field. Philadelphia: J. W. Bradley, 1850.
            W I 80.

*   _____. The Home Mission. . . . Boston:
L. P. Crown and Co.; Philadelphia: J. W. Bradley,
1853.
            W II 100.

_____. Keeping Up Appearances; or, A Tale for
the Rich and Poor. New York: Baker and Scribner,
1848.
            W I 94.

_____. Lizzie Glenn; or, The Trials of a Seam-
stress. Philadelphia: T. B. Peterson and Bros.,
1859.
            W II 107.

*   _____. Love in High Life: A Story of the
"Upper Ten." Philadelphia: T. B. Peterson
[cop. 1849].
            W I 102.

_____. The Maiden: A Story for my Young
Countrywomen. Philadelphia: E. Ferrett and Co.,
1845.
            W I 110.

_____. Mary Ellis; or, The Runaway Match.
Philadelphia: Henry F. Anners [cop. 1850].
            W I 125.

_____. Pride or Principle: Which Makes the
Lady? Philadelphia: Henry F. Anners, 1850.
            W I 140.

* Arthur, Timothy Shay. The Ruined Family, and Other
    Tales . . . In Two Parts. Philadelphia: Godey and
    M'Michael, 1843.
        W I 151.

* _____. Sketches of Life and Character. Phila-
    delphia: J. W. Bradley, 1850.
        W I 162.

* _____. Sparing to Spend; or, The Loftons and
    the Pinkertons. New York: Charles Scribner, 1853.
        W II 125.

  _____. The Two Brides. Philadelphia: T. B.
    Peterson [cop. 1850].
        W I 180.

* _____. What Can Woman Do? Boston: L. P. Crown
    and Co.; Philadelphia: J. W. Bradley, 1855.
        W II 145.

  _____. The Young Music Teacher, and Other
    Tales. N. p., n.d.
        W I 189 (another edition).

Bache, Mrs. Anna. The Fire-Screen; or, Domestic
    Sketches. Philadelphia: W. J. and J. K. Simon,
    1841.
        W I 217.

Badeau, Adam. The Vagabond. New York: Rudd and
    Carleton, 1859.
        W II 173.

[Ballou, Maturin Murray.] Albert Simmons; or, The Mid-
    shipman's Revenge. A Tale of Land and Sea. . . .
    Boston: F. Gleason, 1849.
        W I 229 (another edition).

[_____.] The Gipsey; or, The Robbers of
    Naples. A Story of Love and Pride. . . . Boston:
    F. Gleason, 1847.
        W I 239.

* [_____.] Roderick the Rover; or, The Spirit of
    the Wave. . . . Boston: F. Gleason, 1849.
        W I 251.

Barker, Benjamin. Clarilda; or, The Female Pickpocket.
A Romance of New York City. Boston: F. Gleason,
1846.
      W I 262.

_____. Mornilva; or, The Outlaw of the Forest.
. . . Boston: Gleason's Publishing Hall, 1846.
      W I 274.

Barton, K. Io: A Tale of the Olden Fane. New York:
D. Appleton and Co., 1851.
      W II 232.

* Bennett, Emerson. Rosalie DuPont; or, Treason in the
Camp. A Story of the Revolution. Cincinnati: U. P.
James [cop. 1853].
      W II 282.

* Bickford, Mrs. J. T. Scandal. Boston: Shephard, Clark
and Brown, 1857.
      W II 295.

* [Bickley, Lloyd Wharton.] The Aristocrat: An American
Tale. 2 vols. Philadelphia: Key and Biddle, 1833.
      W I 310.

[Bird, Robert Montgomery.] The Hawks of Hawk-Hollow:
A Tradition of Pennsylvania. 2 vols. Philadelphia:
Carey, Lea and Blanchard, 1835.
      W I 319.

* [_____.] Sheppard Lee. 2 vols. New York:
Harper and Brothers, 1836.
      W I 324.

* [Botsford, Mrs. Margaret.] The Reign of Reform; or,
Yankee Doodle Court. Baltimore: Printed for the
authoress, 1830.
      W I 341.

[Boyce, John.] Mary Lee; or, The Yankee in Ireland.
By Paul Peppergrass. Baltimore: Kelly, Hedian and
Piet; Boston: P. Donahoe, 1860.
      W II 329.

* Bradbury, Osgood. Ellen Grant; or, Fashionable Life in
New York. New York: Dick and Fitzgerald, Printers,
n.d.
      W II 338 (another edition).

* [Bradford, Mrs. Sarah Elizabeth.] <u>Lewie</u>; <u>or</u>, <u>The</u> <u>Bended</u>
   <u>Twig</u>. By <u>Cousin</u> <u>Cicely</u>. Auburn: Alden, Beardsley
   and Co.; Rochester: Wanzer, Beardsley and Co., 1853.
      W II 353.

* <u>The</u> <u>Brigantine</u>; <u>or</u>, <u>Admiral</u> <u>Lowe</u>. <u>A</u> <u>Tale</u> <u>of</u> <u>the</u> <u>Seven</u>-
   <u>teenth</u> <u>Century</u>. . . . New York: Crowen and Decker,
   1839.
      W I 406.

* [Briggs, Emily Edson.] <u>Ellen</u> <u>Parry</u>; <u>or</u>, <u>Trials</u> <u>of</u> <u>the</u>
   <u>Heart</u>. By <u>Olivia</u>. New York: D. Appleton and Co.;
   Philadelphia: Geo. S. Appleton, 1850.
      W I 413.

* [Brown, David.] <u>The</u> <u>Planter</u>; <u>or</u>, <u>Thirteen</u> <u>Years</u> <u>in</u> <u>the</u>
   <u>South</u>. <u>By</u> <u>a</u> <u>Northern</u> <u>Man</u>. Philadelphia: H. Hooker,
   1853.
      W II 377.

* Bryant, John Delavan. <u>Pauline</u> <u>Seward</u>: <u>A</u> <u>Tale</u> <u>of</u> <u>Real</u>
   <u>Life</u>. 2 vols. Baltimore: Printed and published
   by John Murphy; Pittsburg: George Quigley; Dublin:
   R. Grace and Sons, 1847.
      W I 437.

* Buckingham, Henry A. <u>Harry</u> <u>Burnham</u>, <u>The</u> <u>Young</u> <u>Continen</u>-
   <u>tal</u>; <u>or</u>, <u>Memoirs</u> <u>of</u> <u>an</u> <u>American</u> <u>Officer</u> <u>during</u> <u>the</u>
   <u>Campaigns</u> <u>of</u> <u>the</u> <u>Revolution</u>. . . . New York:
   Burgess and Garrett; Baltimore: Burgess, Taylor
   and Co., 1851.
      W II 408.

* [Bunce, Oliver Bell.] <u>Life</u> <u>Before</u> <u>Him</u>: <u>A</u> <u>Novel</u>. New
   York: W. A. Townsend and Co., 1860.
      W II 418.

   Burdett, Charles. <u>Chances</u> <u>and</u> <u>Changes</u>; <u>or</u>, <u>Life</u> <u>as</u> <u>It</u>
   <u>Is</u>: <u>Illustrated</u> <u>in</u> <u>the</u> <u>History</u> <u>of</u> <u>a</u> <u>Straw</u> <u>Hat</u>. New
   York: D. Appleton and Co., 1849.
      W I 450 (another edition).

* Capricorn, Cornelius, pseud. <u>Speculations</u> <u>on</u> <u>the</u> <u>Comet</u>.
   . . . New York: James Kelly, 1832.
      W I 479.

* [Caruthers, William Alexander.] <u>The</u> <u>Kentuckian</u> <u>in</u> <u>New</u>
   <u>York</u>; <u>or</u>, <u>The</u> <u>Adventures</u> <u>of</u> <u>Three</u> <u>Southerns</u>. <u>By</u> <u>a</u>
   <u>Virginian</u>. 2 vols. New York: Harper and Brothers,
   1834.
      W I 494.

Cary, Alice. Married, not Mated; or, How They Lived at
   Woodside and Throckmorton Hall. New York: Derby
   and Jackson; Cincinnati: H. W. Derby, 1856.
      W II 472.

Chesebro', Caroline. Dream-Land by Daylight: A Panorama
   of Romance. New York: Redfield, 1851.
      W II 511.

* Child, Mrs. Lydia Maria. The Coronal: A Collection....
   Boston: Carter and Hendee, 1832.
      W I 516.

* _____. Letters from New York. Second Series.
   New York: C. S. Francis and Co., 1845.
      W I 529.

* [Church, Mrs. Ella Rodman.] The Catanese; or, The Real
   and the Ideal. . . . New York: Bunnell and Price,
   1853.
      W II 524.

Clough, Martha A. Zuleika; or, The Castilian Captive.
   A Romance of the Time of Ferdinand and Isabella.
   Boston: F. Gleason, 1849.
      W I 553.

* Cobb, Joseph Beckham. Mississippi Scenes; or, Sketches
   of Southern and Western Life and Adventure. . . .
   Philadelphia: A. Hart, 1851.
      W II 561.

* Confessions of a Female Inebriate; or, Intemperance in
   High Life. Boston: William Henshaw, 1842.

* [Cooke, John Esten.] Leather Stocking and Silk; or,
   Hunter John Myers and his Times. A Story of the
   Valley of Virginia. New York: Harper and Brothers,
   1854.
      W II 621.

* [Cooper, James Fenimore.] Afloat and Ashore; or, The
   Adventures of Miles Wallingford. . . . 4 vols.
   Philadelphia: Published by the author, 1844.
   Vols. III and IV, New York: Published by the author,
   and for sale by Burgess, Stringer and Co., 1844.
      W I 579.

[Cooper, James Fenimore.] The Deerslayer; or, The First
War-Path. . . . 2 vols. Philadelphia: Lea and
Blanchard, 1841.
W I 589.

* [_____.] Homeward Bound; or, The Chase. . . .
2 vols. Philadelphia: Carey, Lea and Blanchard,
1838.
W I 612.

* _____. Ned Myers; or, A Life before the Mast.
. . . Philadelphia: Lea and Blanchard, 1843.
W I 652.

[_____.] Satanstoe; or, The Littlepage Manu-
scripts. . . . 2 vols. New York: Burgess, Stringer
and Co., 1845.
W I 715.

* [_____.] The Ways of the Hour. New York:
George P. Putnam, 1850.
W I 744.

The Cooper's Son; or, The Prize of Virtue. A Tale of the
Revolution. . . . Boston: James French, 1846.
W I 761.

Cox, William. Crayon Sketches. By an Amateur. . . .
2 vols. New York: Conner and Cooke, 1833.
W I 771.

* Cozzens, Frederick Swartwout. The Sparrowgrass Papers;
or, Living in the Country. New York: Derby and
Jackson; Cincinnati: H. W. Derby, 1856.
W II 652.

[Curtis, George William.] The Potiphar Papers. . . .
New York: G. P. Putnam and Co., 1853.
W II 676.

* [Curtis, Harriot F.] Jessie's Flirtations. . . . New
York: Harper and Brothers, 1846.
W I 780.

Curtis, Newton Mallory. The Patrol of the Mountain.
A Tale of the Revolution. New York: W. F. Burgess;
Cincinnati: Burgess and Ward, 1849.
W I 803 (another edition).

* [Davis, Charles Augustus.] Letters of J. Downing, Major,
   Downingville Militia, Second Brigade, to his Old
   Friend, Mr. Dwight, of the New-York Daily Advertiser.
   New York: Harper and Brothers, 1834.
        W I 827.

Denison, Mrs. Mary A. The Days and Ways of the Cocked
   Hats; or, The Dawn of the Revolution. New York:
   S. A. Rollo, 1860.
        W II 721.

The Diary of a Pawnbroker; or, The Three Golden Balls.
   New York: H. Long and Brother [cop. 1849].
        W I 852.

* Dixon, Edward H., M.D. Scenes in the Practice of a New
   York Surgeon. New York: Robert M. DeWitt [cop.
   1855].
        W II 758.

The Dream Fulfilled; or, The Trials and Triumphs of the
   Moreland Family. Boston: James French, 1846.
        W I 863.

* Dupuy, Eliza Ann. The Conspirator. New York: D. Appleton and Co.; Philadelphia: Geo. S. Appleton, 1850.
        W I 877.

* [_____.] The Huguenot Exiles; or, The Times of
   Louis XIV. . . . New York: Harper and Brothers,
   1856.
        W II 819.

[Durivage, Francis Alexander, and Burnham, George P.]
   Stray Subjects, Arrested and Bound Over. . . .
   Philadelphia: T. B. Peterson and Brothers [cop.
   1848].
        W I 886 (another edition).

* Eastman, Mrs. Mary H. Aunt Phillis's Cabin; or, Southern
   Life as It Is. . . . Philadelphia: Lippincott,
   Grambo and Co., 1852.
        W II 831.

_____. Dahcotah; or, Life and Legends of the
   Sioux Around Fort Snelling. . . . New York: John
   Wiley, 1849.
        W I 890.

* [Elliott, Samuel Hayes.] The Sequel to Rolling Ridge.
      . . . Boston: Published by Crocker and Brewster,
      1844.
            W I 904.

English, William B. Rosina Meadows, the Village Maid;
      or, Temptations Unveiled. . . . [Boston: Redding
      and Co., 1843.]
            W I 917. T. p. wanting in UP copy.

* Estelle Grant; or, The Lost Wife. New York: Garrett and
      Co. [cop. 1855].

* Farnham, Eliza Woodson. Life in Prairie Land. . . . New
      York: Harper and Brothers, 1846.

* Farrenc, Edmund. Carlotina and the Sanfedisti; or,
      A Night with the Jesuits at Rome. New York: John S.
      Taylor, 1853.
            W II 889.

* [Fay, Theodore Sedgwick.] Norman Leslie: A Tale of the
      Present Times. New York: Harper and Brothers, 1835.
            W I 936.

* Florence DeLacey; or, The Coquette. . . . New York:
      E. Winchester, New World Press, n.d.
            W I 964 (another edition).

* Forbes, Gerritt Van Husen. Green Mountain Annals: A Tale
      of Truth. New York: Burnett and Smith, 1832.
            W I 972.

* Foster, George G. New York Naked. . . . New York:
      DeWitt and Davenport, n.d.
            W II 937.

[Fox, Mary Anna.] George Allen, the Only Son. . . .
      Boston: William Peirce, 1835.
            W I 999.

Frink, Henry C. Alow and Aloft, On Board and on Shore.
      Rochester: William Alling, 1842.
            W I 1013.

[Gilman, Mrs. Caroline.] Recollections of a Housekeeper.
      . . . New York: Harper and Brothers, 1836.
            W I 1026.

[Goodrich, Samuel Griswold.] <u>Moral</u> <u>Tales</u>; <u>or</u>, <u>A</u> <u>Selec-tion</u> <u>of</u> <u>Interesting</u> <u>Stories</u>. <u>By</u> <u>the</u> <u>Author</u> <u>of</u> <u>Peter</u> <u>Parley</u>. Vol. I. New York: Nafis and Cornish [1840].
    W I 1041.

[_____.] <u>A</u> <u>Tale</u> <u>of</u> <u>Adventure</u>; <u>or</u>, <u>The</u> <u>Siberian</u> <u>Sable</u> <u>Hunter</u>. . . . New York: Wiley and Putnam, 1844.
    W I 1044 (another edition).

Graves, Mrs. A. J. <u>Girlhood</u> <u>and</u> <u>Womanhood</u>; <u>or</u>, <u>Sketches</u> <u>of</u> <u>my</u> <u>Schoolmates</u>. Boston: T. H. Carter and Co., and Benjamin Mussey, 1844.
    W I 1055.

* [Greene, Asa.] <u>The</u> <u>Perils</u> <u>of</u> <u>Pearl</u> <u>Street</u>; <u>Including</u> <u>a</u> <u>Taste</u> <u>of</u> <u>the</u> <u>Dangers</u> <u>of</u> <u>Wall</u> <u>Street</u>. <u>By</u> <u>a</u> <u>Late</u> <u>Merchant</u>. New York: Betts and Anstice, and Peter Hill, 1834.
    W I 1066.

[Greenough, Henry.] <u>Apelles</u> <u>and</u> <u>his</u> <u>Contemporaries</u>: <u>A</u> <u>Novel</u>. Boston: T. O. H. P. Burnham, 1860.
    W II 1023.

* [Griffith, Mrs. Mary.] <u>Our</u> <u>Neighbourhood</u>; <u>or</u>, <u>Letters</u> <u>on</u> <u>Horticultural</u> <u>and</u> <u>Natural</u> <u>Phenomena</u>. . . . New York: E. Bliss, 1831.
    W I 1072.

* [Hale, Mrs. Sara Josepha.] "<u>Boarding</u> <u>Out</u>." <u>A</u> <u>Tale</u> <u>of</u> <u>Domestic</u> <u>Life</u>. New York: Harper and Brothers, 1846.
    W I 1079.

Hall, James. <u>The</u> <u>Harpe's</u> <u>Head</u>: <u>A</u> <u>Legend</u> <u>of</u> <u>Kentucky</u>. Philadelphia: Key and Biddle, 1833.
    W I 1097.

* _____. <u>The</u> <u>Wilderness</u> <u>and</u> <u>the</u> <u>War</u> <u>Path</u>. New York: Wiley and Putnam, 1846.
    W I 1102.

* Hall, Mrs. Louisa Jane. <u>Miriam</u>, <u>and</u> <u>Joanna</u> <u>of</u> <u>Naples</u>, <u>with</u> <u>Other</u> <u>Pieces</u> <u>in</u> <u>Verse</u> <u>and</u> <u>Prose</u>. Boston: Wm. Crosby and H. P. Nichols, 1850.
    W I 1107.

* Hammond, Samuel H., and Mansfield, L. W. Country Margins
      and Rambles of a Journalist. New York: J. C. Derby,
      1855.
              W II 1084.

[Hare, Robert.] Standish the Puritan: A Tale of the
      American Revolution. . . . New York: Harper and
      Brothers, 1850.
              W I 1128.

Haven, Mrs. Alice Emily Neal. The Gossips of Rivertown:
      With Sketches in Prose and Verse. . . . Philadel-
      phia: Hazard and Mitchell, 1850.
              W I 1136.

Hawthorne, Nathaniel. The House of Seven Gables: A Ro-
      mance. Boston: Ticknor, Reed and Fields, 1851.
              W II 1135.

_____ . The Scarlet Letter: A Romance. Boston:
      Ticknor, Reed and Fields, 1850.
              W I 1146.

Hazen, Jacob A. Five Years before the Mast; or, Life in
      the Forecastle aboard of a Whaler and Man-of-War.
      Philadelphia: Willis P. Hazard, 1854.
              W II 1145.

* Hentz, Mrs. Caroline Lee. The Lost Daughter, and Other
      Stories of the Heart. Philadelphia: T. B. Peterson
      [cop. 1857].
              W II 1160.

* Herbert, Henry William. The Chevaliers of France, from
      the Crusaders to the Marechals of Louis XIV. New
      York: Redfield, 1853.
              W II 1170.

[_____ .] The Deerstalkers; or, Circumstantial
      Evidence. . . . Philadelphia: Carey and Hart, 1849.
              W I 1162.

_____ . Marmaduke Wyvil; or, The Maid's
      Revenge. New York: J. Winchester, New World Press
      [cop. 1843].
              W I 1169.

* _____ . Tales of the Spanish Seas. New York:
      Burgess, Stringer and Co., 1847.
              W I 1179.

Herbert, Henry William. <u>Wager</u> <u>of</u> <u>Battle</u>: <u>A</u> <u>Tale</u> <u>of</u> <u>Saxon</u>
<u>Slavery</u> <u>in</u> <u>Sherwood</u> <u>Forest</u>. New York: Mason Broth-
ers, 1855.
     W II 1174.

Hill, George Canning. <u>Our</u> <u>Parish</u>; <u>or,</u> <u>Annals</u> <u>of</u> <u>Pastor</u>
<u>and</u> <u>People</u>. Boston: L. P. Crown and Co.; Philadel-
phia: J. W. Bradley, 1854.
     W II 1210.

* Hine, E. Curtiss. <u>Orlando</u> <u>Melville</u>; <u>or,</u> <u>The</u> <u>Victims</u> <u>of</u>
<u>the</u> <u>Press-gang</u>. . . . Boston: F. Gleason [cop.
1848].
     W I 1194.

* Holbrook, Silas P. <u>Sketches,</u> <u>by</u> <u>a</u> <u>Traveller</u>. Boston:
Carter and Hendee, 1830.
     W I 1221

* Holmes, Mrs. Mary Jane. <u>Dora</u> <u>Deane</u>; <u>or,</u> <u>The</u> <u>East</u> <u>India</u>
<u>Uncle</u>. And <u>Maggie</u> <u>Miller</u>; <u>or,</u> <u>Old</u> <u>Hagar's</u> <u>Secret</u>.
New York: C. M. Saxton, 1859.
     W II 1236.

* [Hornblower, Mrs. Jane Elizabeth.] <u>Vara</u>; <u>or,</u> <u>The</u> <u>Daugh-</u>
<u>ter</u> <u>of</u> <u>Adoption</u>. New York: Robert Carter and Broth-
ers, 1854.
     W II 1268.

* [Hubbell, Mrs. Martha.] <u>The</u> <u>Shady</u> <u>Side</u>; <u>or,</u> <u>Life</u> <u>in</u> <u>a</u>
<u>Country</u> <u>Parsonage</u>. Boston: John P. Jewett; Cleve-
land: Jewett, Proctor and Worthington; London: Low
and Co., 1853.
     W II 1292.

* <u>Humorist</u> <u>Tales</u>: <u>Being</u> <u>a</u> <u>Selection</u> <u>of</u> <u>Interesting</u> <u>Tales</u>.
. . . New York: Nafis and Cornish; St. Louis:
Nafis, Cornish and Co. [cop. 1841].
     W I 1242 (another edition).

* Huntington, Jedediah Vincent. <u>Rosemary</u>; <u>or,</u> <u>Life</u> <u>and</u>
<u>Death</u>. New York, Boston, Montreal: D. and J.
Sadlier and Co., 1860.
     W II 1312.

* [Ingraham, Joseph Holt.] <u>The</u> <u>American</u> <u>Lounger</u>; <u>or,</u>
<u>Tales,</u> <u>Sketches</u> <u>and</u> <u>Legends</u>. . . . Philadelphia:
Lea and Blanchard, 1839.
     W I 1257.

* [Ingraham, Joseph Holt.] Captain Kyd: or, The Wizard of
the Sea. 2 vols. New York: Harper and Brothers,
1839.
     W I 1273.

* _____. The Dancing Feather; or, The Amateur
Freebooters. A Romance of New York. Boston: George
Roberts, 1842.
     W I 1279.

* _____. The Gipsy of the Highlands; or, The Jew
and the Heir. . . . Boston: Redding and Co., 1843.
     W I 1297.

* _____. Jemmy Daily; or, The Little News
Vender. . . . Boston: Brainerd and Co., 1843.
     W I 1306.

[_____.] "Lame Davy's Son, with the Birth,
Education, and Career, of Foraging Peter." Boston
Notion, Extra series, Vol. I, nos. 9 and 10.

_____. Morris Graeme; or, The Cruise of the
Sea-Slipper. A Sequel to The Dancing Feather.
[Boston: E. P. Williams, 1843.]
     W I 1327. Title page wanting in UP copy.

_____. Rafael; or, The Twice Condemned. A Tale
of Key West. Boston: H. L. Williams, at the
"Yankee" Office, 1845.
     W I 1338.

* [_____.] The South-West. By a Yankee. 2 vols.
New York: Harper and Brothers, 1835.
     W I 1349.

Irving, John Treat, Jr. The Hawk Chief: A Tale of the
Indian Country. 2 vols. Philadelphia: Carey, Lea
and Blanchard, 1837.
     W I 1368.

[Irving, Washington.] A Book of the Hudson: Collected
from the Various Works of Diedrich Knickerbocker.
Edited by Geoffrey Crayon. New York: G. P. Putnam,
1849.
     W I 1378.

_____. Wolfert's Roost, and Other Papers, Now
First Collected. . . . New York: G. P. Putnam and
Co., 1855.
     W II 1327.

* Isabel; or, The Trials of the Heart. A Tale for the
  Young. . . . New York: Harper and Brothers, 1845.
      W I 1460.

  Jarves, James Jackson. Why and What Am I? The Confes-
    sions of an Inquirer, in Three Parts. Part I, Heart-
    Experience. . . . Boston: Phillips, Sampson and
    Co.; London: Sampson Low, Son, and Co., 1857.
      W II 1341.

* Jerauld, Mrs. Charlotte A. Poetry and Prose: With a
    Memoir, by Henry Bacon. Boston: A. Tompkins, 1850.
      W I 1468.

* Jones, John Beauchamp. Life and Adventures of a Country
    Merchant. . . . Philadelphia: Lippincott, Grambo
    and Co., 1854.
      W II 1373.

* _____. Wild Western Scenes: A Narrative of
    Adventures in the Western Wilderness, Forty Years
    Ago. . . . Philadelphia: E. Ferrett and Co., 1845.
      W I 1478.

* [Jones, Justin.] Mad Jack and Gentleman Jack; or, The
    Last Cruise of Old Ironsides around the World. . . .
    Boston: Star Spangled Banner Office, 1850.
      W I 1495.

  [_____.] Red Ruthven; or, Love, War, and
    Treachery. . . . Boston: Star Spangled Banner
    Office, 1848.

* Jones, Pascal. My Uncle Hobson and I; or, Slashes at
    Life with a Free Broad-Axe. New York: D. Appleton
    and Co.; Philadelphia: Geo. S. Appleton, 1845.
      W I 1507.

* [Judd, Sylvester.] Margaret: A Tale of the Real and the
    Ideal, Blight and Bloom. . . . Rev. ed., 2 vols.
    Boston: Phillips, Sampson and Co., 1857.
      W II 1410 (another edition).

  [Judson, Edward Zane Carroll.] The Black Avenger of the
    Spanish Main. A Thrilling Story of the Buccaneer
    Times. By Ned Buntline. Boston: F. Gleason's Pub-
    lishing Hall, 1852.
      W I 1515 (another edition).

* [Judson, Edward Zane Carroll.] The Volunteer; or, The
    Maid of Monterrey. A Tale of the Mexican War. By Ned
    Buntline. Boston: F. Gleason, The Flag of Our Union
    Office, 1847.
        W I 1537.

* [Judson, Mrs. Emily.] Trippings in Author-Land. By Fanny
    Forester. New York: Paine and Burgess, 1846.
        W I 1558.

[Kennedy, John Pendleton.] Swallow Barn; or, A Sojourn
    in the Old Dominion. 2 vols. Philadelphia: Carey
    and Lea, 1832.
        W I 1569.

[Kilbourn, Diana Treat.] The Lone Dove: A Legend of
    Revolutionary Times. Philadelphia: Geo. S. Appleton;
    New York: D. Appleton and Co., 1850.
        W I 1576.

* Kirkland, Mrs. Caroline Matilda. Western Clearings. New
    York: Wiley and Putnam, 1845.
        W I 1587.

* The Knickerbocker Gallery: A Testimonial to the Editor of
    the Knickerbocker Magazine. . . . New York: Samuel
    Hueston, 1855.
        W II 1492.

[Lee, Mrs. Eliza Buckminster.] Delusion; or, The Witch
    of New England. Boston: Hilliard, Grey and Co.,
    1840.
        W I 1608.

—————————————. Parthenia; or, The Last Days of Pagan-
    ism. Boston: Ticknor and Fields, 1858.
        W II 1525.

[Lee, Mrs. Hannah Farnham.] The Contrast; or, Modes of
    Education. . . . Boston: Whipple and Damrell, 1837.
        W I 1613.

[—————————————.] Rich Enough: A Tale of the Times.
    Boston: Whipple and Damrell, 1837.
        W I 1630.

[—————————————.] Worth a Million: Stories From Real
    Life, Part V. New York: S. Colman; Boston: Weeks,
    Jordan and Co., 1838.

Leslie, Eliza. <u>Laura Lovel</u>: A <u>Sketch</u>--<u>for</u> <u>Ladies</u> <u>Only</u>.
 Lowell: Published at the Franklin Bookstore, 1834.
  W I 1651.

* _____. <u>Pencil</u> <u>Sketches</u>; <u>or</u>, <u>Outlines</u> <u>of</u> <u>Char</u>-
 <u>acter</u> <u>and</u> <u>Manners</u>. . . . <u>Second</u> <u>Series</u>. Philadelphia: Carey, Lea and Blanchard, 1835.
  W I 1656.

* Lippard, George. <u>Legends</u> <u>of</u> <u>Mexico</u>. Philadelphia: T. B.
 Peterson, 1847.
  W I 1684.

* [Lippincott, Mrs. Sara Jane.] <u>Greenwood</u> <u>Leaves</u>: A <u>Col</u>-
 <u>lection</u> <u>of</u> <u>Sketches</u> <u>and</u> <u>Letters</u>. <u>By</u> <u>Grace</u> <u>Greenwood</u>.
 Boston: Ticknor, Reed and Fields, 1850.
  W I 1697.

* [_____.] <u>Greenwood</u> <u>Leaves</u>. . . . <u>Second</u>
 <u>Series</u>. Boston: Ticknor, Reed and Fields, 1852.
  W II 1559.

[Lockwood, Ralph Ingersoll.] <u>Rosine</u> <u>Laval</u>: A <u>Novel</u>.
 Philadelphia. Carey, Lea and Blanchard, 1833.
  W I 1706.

[Longstreet, Augustus Baldwin.] <u>Georgia</u> <u>Scenes</u>, <u>Charac</u>-
 <u>ters</u>, <u>Incidents</u>, <u>&c</u>., <u>in</u> <u>the</u> <u>First</u> <u>Half</u> <u>Century</u> <u>of</u>
 <u>the</u> <u>Republic</u>. Augusta: Printed at the S. R. Senti-
 nel Office, 1835.
  W I 1721.

[Lunt, George.] <u>Eastford</u>; <u>or</u>, <u>Household</u> <u>Sketches</u>. Boston: Crocker and Brewster, 1855.
  W II 1595.

* [McClung, John Alexander.] <u>Camden</u>: <u>A</u> <u>Tale</u> <u>of</u> <u>the</u> <u>South</u>.
 2 vols. Philadelphia: Carey and Lea, 1830.
  W I 1744.

* [McDowell, J. R.] <u>Henry</u> <u>Wallace</u>; <u>or</u>, <u>The</u> <u>Victim</u> <u>of</u> <u>Lot</u>-
 <u>tery</u> <u>Gambling</u>. <u>A</u> <u>Moral</u> <u>Tale</u>. New York: Printed and
 published by Wilson and Swain, 1832.
  W I 1748.

[McIntosh, Maria Jane.] <u>Conquest</u> <u>and</u> <u>Self-Conquest</u>; <u>or</u>,
 <u>Which</u> <u>Makes</u> <u>the</u> <u>Hero</u>? New York: Harper and Brothers,
 1843.
  W I 1762.

MacKenzie, Robert Shelton. Tressilian and his Friends. Philadelphia: J. B. Lippincott and Co., 1859. W II 1637.

* [Mallory, Daniel.] Short Stories and Reminiscences of the Last Fifty Years. 4th ed., 2 vols. New York: Dan'l Mallory; R. P. Bixby and Co.; Philadelphia: Carey and Hart; Boston: Jordan and Co., 1842. W I 1783.

Mancur, John Henry. Everard Norton. [New York: William H. Colyer, 1843.] W I 1789. Title page wanting in UP copy.

* Marsh, John. Hannah Hawkins, the Reformed Drunkard's Daughter. New York: American Temperance Union, 1844. W I 1814.

Mathews, Cornelius. The Career of Puffer Hopkins. Included in Mathews, The Various Writings . . . , below.

_____. The Various Writings. . . . New York: Harper and Brothers, 1843. W I 1837.

* [Mathews, Julia A.] Lily Huson; or, Early Struggles 'Midst Continual Hope. . . . New York: H. Long and Brother [cop. 1855]. W II 1683.

[Mayo, Mrs. Sara Carter.] The Palfreys: A Tale. Boston: Abel Tompkins, 1838. W I 1846.

* Means without Living. . . . Boston: Weeks, Jordan and Co., 1837. W I 1857.

[Meeker, Nathan Cook.] Life and Adventures of Captain Jacob B. Armstrong. New York: DeWitt and Davenport, 1852. W II 1693.

* Melville, Herman. The Piazza Tales. New York: Dix and Edwards; London: Sampson Low, Son and Co., 1856. W II 1702.

* Melville, Herman. _Typee: A Peep at Polynesian Life_.
  New York: Wiley and Putnam; London: John Murray,
  1846.
  > W I 1867.

[Mitchell, John.] _Rachel Kell_. New York: M. W. Dodd,
  1853.
  > W II 1724.

Miss Eliza Rossell: A Tale of the Unfortunate Female.
  . . . Boston: Z. D. Montague, 1845.
  > W I 1879.

[Moore, John McDermott.] _Lord Nial: A Romance_. . . .
  New York: John Doyle, 1834.
  > W I 1914.

Morgan, Nathan Denison. _George Cardwell; or, A Month
  in a Country Parish_. New York: Dana and Co., 1856.
  > W II 1749.

* [Motley, John Lothrop.] _Merry-Mount: A Romance of the
  Massachusetts Colony_. 2 vols. Boston and Cam-
  bridge: James Munroe and Co., 1849.
  > W I 1926.

Myers, Peter Hamilton. _The Miser's Heir; or, The Young
  Millionaire_. Philadelphia: T. B. Peterson [cop.
  1854].
  > W II 1773.

[_____.] _The Young Patroon; or, Christmas
  in 1690_. . . . New York: George P. Putnam; London:
  Putnam's American Agency, 1849.
  > W I 1936.

Neal, Joseph Clay. _Charcoal Sketches; or, Scenes in
  a Metropolis_. 3d ed. Philadelphia: E. L. Carey
  and A. Hart, 1839.
  > W I 1953.

* Nichols, Thomas Low. _Raffle for a Wife_. New York:
  Burgess, Stringer and Co., 1845.
  > W I 1968.

Nowell, Sarah Allen. _The Shadow on the Pillow, and Other
  Stories_. Boston: A. Tompkins, 1860.
  > W II 1806.

* Oran, The Outcast; or, A Season in New York.   2 vols.
     New York: Peabody and Co., 1833.
          W I 1981.

* Otis, Eliza Henderson.   The Barclays of Boston.   Boston:
     Ticknor, Reed and Fields, 1854.
          W II 1828.

* Paul Jones: A Tale of the Sea. . . .   Philadelphia:
     A. J. Rockafellar, 1843.
          W I 1996.

* [Parton, Mrs. Sara Payson.]   Fresh Leaves. By Fanny Fern.
     New York: Mason Brothers, 1857.
          W II 1847.

  [Paulding, James Kirke.]   The Old Continental; or,
     The Price of Liberty.   2 vols. New York: Paine
     and Burgess, 1846.
          W I 2018.

* [Pearson, Mrs. Emily.]   Cousin Franck's Household; or,
     Scenes in the Old Dominion. . . .   Boston: Upham,
     Ford and Olmstead, 1853.
          W II 1856.

  [Peck, George Washington.]   Aurifodina; or, Adventures
     in the Gold Region. By Cantell A. Bigly.   New York:
     Baker and Scribner, 1849.
          W I 2030.

* [Phelps, Mrs. Elizabeth.]   The Tell-Tale; or, Home
     Secrets Told by Old Travellers. . . .   Boston:
     Phillips, Sampson and Co., 1853.
          W II 1887.

  The Philosophical Emperor: A Political Experiment. . . .
     New York: Harper and Brothers, 1841.
          W I 2043.

  [Poe, Edgar Allan.]   The Narrative of Arthur Gordon Pym
     of Nantucket. . . .   New York: Harper and Brothers,
     1838.
          W I 2052.

* The Polish Chiefs: An Historical Romance.   2 vols.   New
     York: J. K. Porter, 1832.
          W I 2058.

Poore, Benjamin Perley. The Mameluke; or, The Sign of
the Mystic Tie. A Tale of the Camp and Court of
Bonaparte. Boston: F. Gleason's Publishing Hall,
1852.
W II 1928.

* [Price, William.] Clement Falconer; or, The Memoirs of
a Young Whig. 2 vols. Baltimore: N. Hickman, 1838.
W I 2072.

[Prime, William Cowper.] The Old House by the River.
New York: Harper and Brothers, 1853.
W II 1963.

* Recollections of the United States Army: A Series of
Thrilling Tales and Sketches. By an American Sol-
dier. . . . Boston: James Munroe and Co., 1845.
W I 2105.

* Remarkable Narrative of the Female Hermit: And Teloula,
The Indian Girl. Boston, 1849.
W I 1670.

* [Reynolds, Elhanan Winchester.] Records of the Bubbleton
Parish; or, Papers from the Experience of an American Minister. Boston: A. Tompkins and B. B. Mussey
and Co., 1854.
W II 2019.

* Riley, Henry Hiram. The Puddleford Papers; or, Humors of
the West. New York: Derby and Jackson; Cincinnati:
H. W. Derby and Co., 1857.
W II 2044.

* [Ritchie, Mrs. Anna Cora Mowatt.] The Fortune Hunter;
or, The Adventures of a Man about Town. A Novel of
New York Society. . . . New York: J. Winchester,
New World Press, [cop. 1844].
W I 2121.

Robinson, James Hovey. The Silver Bell; or, The Heir of
Motcombe Manor. A Romance of Merry England. Boston:
F. Gleason's Publishing Hall, 1853.
W II 2085.

[Robinson, Mrs. Therese Albertine Louise.] Heloise; or,
The Unrevealed Secret. A Tale by Talvi. New York:
D. Appleton and Co., 1850.
W I 2142.

Roe, Azel Stevens. To Love and Be Loved: And Time and
    Tide; or, Strive and Win. New York: Derby and Jack-
    son, 1858.
        W II 2011 (Time and Tide is the title in the
            sample).

Rosewood, Miss Emma. Alford and Selina; or, The Mystery
    Disclosed, and the Reputed Orphan Restored. . . .
    Boston: Dow and Jackson, 1845.
        W I 2157.

* Russell, Martha. Leaves from the Tree Igdrasyl. Boston:
    John P. Jewett; Cleveland: Jewett, Proctor and Worth-
    ington; New York: Sheldon, Lamport and Blakeman,
    1854.
        W II 2143.

The Salem Belle: A Tale of 1692. Boston: Tappan and
    Dennet, 1842.
        W I 2272.

Sargent, Lucius Manlius. My Mother's Gold Ring.
    15th ed. Boston: Ford and Damrell, 1833.
        W I 2295.

* [_____.] The Stage-Coach. Founded on Fact.
    2d ed. Boston: Whipple and Damrell; New York:
    Schofield and Voorhies, 1838.
        W I 2301.

[Sawyer, Lemuel.] Printz Hall: A Record of New Sweden.
    2 vols. Philadelphia: Carey and Hart, Hogan and
    Thompson, Thomas, Cowperthwaite and Co., Grigg and
    Elliott; New York: C. and G. Carvill, Harper and
    Brothers, 1839.
        W I 2318.

* Sealsfield, Charles (Karl Anton Postl). Life in the New
    World; or, Sketches of American Society. New York:
    J. Winchester, New World Press [cop. 1844].
        W I 2329.

Sears, Edmund Hamilton. Pictures of the Olden Time, as
    Shown in the Fortunes of a Family of the Pilgrims.
    Boston: Crosby, Nichols and Co.; Cincinnati: George
    S. Blanchard; London: Sampson Low, Son and Co.,
    1857.
        W II 2174.

* [Sedgwick, Catharine Maria.] Clarence; or, A Tale of Our
     Own Times. 2 vols. Philadelphia: Carey and Lea,
     1830.
          W I 2339.

  [_____.] The Poor Rich Man, and the Rich Poor
     Man. New York: Harper and Brothers, 1836.
          W I 2358.

  [Sedgwick, Mrs. Susan Anne.] Allen Prescott; or, The
     Fortunes of a New England Boy. 2 vols. New York:
     Harper and Brothers, 1834.
          W I 2374.

* Shadow, Ben (pseud.). Echoes of a Belle; or, A Voice
     from the Past. New York: George P. Putnam and Co.,
     1853.
          W II 2192.

  Shillaber, Benjamin Penhallow. Knitting-Work: A Web of
     Many Textures. . . . Boston: Brown, Taggard and
     Chase; New York: Sheldon and Co.; Philadelphia:
     J. B. Lippincott and Co., 1859.
          W II 2207.

* Shindler, Mrs. Mary Stanley Bunce. The Young Sailor:
     A Narrative Founded on Fact. New York: Harper and
     Brothers, 1843.
          W I 2385.

  Sigourney, Mrs. Lydia Howard. Myrtis: With Other Etch-
     ings and Sketchings. New York: Harper and Brothers
     [cop. 1846].
          W I 2395.

  [Simms, William Gilmore.] Beauchampe; or, The Kentucky
     Tragedy. A Tale of Passion. 2 vols. Philadelphia:
     Lea and Blanchard, 1842.
          W I 2407. UP holds Vol. I only.

  _____. The Cassique of Accabee. . . . New
     York: Geo. P. Putnam, 1849.

* _____. The Cassique of Kiawah: A Colonial
     Romance. New York: Redfield, 1859.
          W II 2221.

  _____. Father Abbot; or, The Home Tourist.
     . . . Charleston: Printed by Miller and Browne,
     1849.
          W I 2418.

[Simms, William Gilmore.] The Golden Christmas: A Chron-
     icle of St. John's, Berkeley. . . . Charleston:
     Walker, Richards and Co., 1852.
          W II 2225.

* [_____.] The Kinsmen; or, The Black Riders of
     the Congaree. 2 vols. Philadelphia: Lea and
     Blanchard, 1841.
          W I 2425.

* [_____.] The Partisan: A Tale of the Revolu-
     tion. 2 vols. New York: Harper and Brothers, 1835.
          W I 2431.

  [_____.] Vasconselos: A Romance of the New
     World. New York: Redfield, 1853.
          W II 2232.

  [_____.] The Wigwam and the Cabin. Second
     Series. New York: Wiley and Putnam, 1845.
          W I 2437.

Smith, Mrs. Elizabeth Oakes. Riches without Wings; or,
     The Cleveland Family. Boston and New York: George
     W. Light, 1838.
          W I 2450.

Smith, J. N. The Way of the World; or, Honesty the Best
     Policy. A Tale of New England and New York. Dedham:
     Printed by Cox and Hutchins, 1854.
          W II 2261.

[Smith, Seba.] John Smith's Letters, with "Picters" to
     Match. New York: Samuel Colman, 1839.
          W I 2464.

[Smith, William Russell.] As It Is. Albany: Munsell and
     Rowland, 1860.
          W II 2279.

* Snelling, Mrs. Anna L. Kabaosa; or, The Warriors of the
     West. A Tale of the Last War. New York: Printed for
     the publisher by D. Adee, 1842.
          W I 2476.

* Southworth, Mrs. Emma Dorothy Eliza Nevitte. The Curse
     of Clifton. Philadelphia: T. B. Peterson and
     Brothers [cop. 1852].
          W II 2301 (another edition).

* Southworth, Mrs. Emma Dorothy Eliza Nevitte. The Mother-
    in-Law: A Tale of Domestic Life. Philadelphia:
    T. B. Peterson and Brothers [cop. 1860].
        W II 2318 (another edition).

[Spofford, Mrs. Harriet Elizabeth.] Sir Rohan's Ghost:
    A Romance. Boston: J. E. Tilton and Co., 1860.
        W II 2341.

* Spofford, Harry. The Mysteries of Worcester; or, Charley
    Temple and his First Glass of Liquor. A Temperance
    Tale. Worcester: H. J. Copp, 1846.
        W I 2485.

* Stephens, Mrs. Ann Sophia. Fashion and Famine. New
    York: Bunce and Brother, 1854.
        W II 2358.

* [_____.] High Life in New York. By Jonathan
    Slick, Esq. [New York: Edward Stephens, 1843].
        W I 2498. Title page wanting in UP copy.

Stephens, Mrs. Harriet Marion. Hagar the Martyr; or,
    Passion and Reality. A Tale of the North and South.
    Boston: W. P. Fetridge and Co., 1855.
        W II 2377.

* [Stone, William Leete.] Ups and Downs in the Life of
    a Distressed Gentleman. New York: Leavitt, Lord
    and Co.; Boston: Crocker and Brewster, 1836.
        W I 2510.

* Stowe, Mrs. Harriet Beecher. Uncle Sam's Emancipation;
    Earthly Care, a Heavenly Discipline; and Other
    Sketches. Philadelphia: Willis P. Hazard, 1853.
        W II 2400.

* Swell Life at Sea; or, Fun, Frigates and Yachting. . . .
    New York: Stringer and Townsend, 1854.
        W II 2414.

Talbot, Mary Elizabeth. Rurality: Original Desultory
    Tales. Providence: Marshall and Hammond, Printers,
    1830.
        W I 2526.

* [Terhune, Mrs. Mary Virginia.] Nemesis. New York: Derby
    and Jackson, 1860.
        W II 2450.

* [Thomas, Frederick William.] Clinton Bradshaw; or, The
    Adventures of a Lawyer. 2 vols. Philadelphia:
    Carey, Lea and Blanchard, 1835.
        W I 2559.

* _____. Sketches of Character, and Tales
    Founded on Fact. Louisville: The Chronicle of
    Western Literature and Art, 1849.
        W I 2563.

Thompson, Daniel Pierce. Lucy Hosmer; or, The Guardian
    and the Ghost. A Tale of Avarice and Crime Defeated.
    Burlington: C. Goodrich and S. B. Nichols, 1848.
        W I 2575.

* Thompson, George. The Brazen Star; or, The Adventures
    of a New York M. P. A True Tale of the Times We Live
    In. New York: George W. Hill, 1853.
        W II 2478.

* [Thomson, Mortimer Neal.] Doesticks' Letters; and What
    He Says. Philadelphia: T. B. Peterson and Brothers
    [cop. 1855].
        W II 2493 (another edition).

The Thrilling and Romantic Story of Sarah Smith and the
    Hessian: An Original Tale of the American Revolu-
    tion. . . . Philadelphia, 1845.
        W I 2599.

* Throop, George Higby. Lynde Weiss: An Autobiography.
    Philadelphia: Lippincott, Grambo and Co., 1852.
        W II 2501.

* [Townsend, Frederic.] Spiritual Visitors. New York:
    John S. Taylor, 1854.
        W II 2531.

* Tucker, St. George. Hansford: A Tale of Bacon's Rebel-
    lion. Richmond: George M. West, 1857.
        W II 2558.

* Tuckerman, Henry Theodore. Isabel; or, Sicily. A Pil-
    grimage. Philadelphia: Lea and Blanchard, 1839.
        W I 2614.

* [Tuthill, Mrs. Louisa Caroline.] The Belle, the Blue,
    and the Bigot; or, Three Fields for Woman's Influ-
    ence. Providence: Samuel C. Blodgett, 1844.
        W I 2624.

Vide, V. V. Sketches of Aboriginal Life. . . . New
    York: Buckland and Sumner, 1846.
        W I 2641.

* Vidi (pseud.) Mr. Frank, the Underground Mail-Agent.
    Philadelphia: Lippincott, Grambo and Co., 1853.
        W II 2593.

[Ware, William.] Julian; or, Scenes in Judea. 2d ed.,
    2 vols. New York: C. S. Francis, and Co., 1856.
        W I 2656 (another edition).

* [Warner, Susan Bogert.] The Hills of the Shatemuc.
    New York: D. Appleton and Co., 1856.
        W II 2646.

Warren, Grenliffe. Olph; or, The Wreckers of the Isle
    of Shoals. A Romance of Sixty Years Ago. Boston:
    H. L. Williams, 1846.
        W I 2672.

* Webber, Charles Wilkins. Tales of the Southern Border.
    Philadelphia: Lippincott, Grambo and Co., 1853.
        W II 2c72.

Weld, Horatio Hastings. Jonce Smiley, the Yankee Boy
    Who Had No Friends. . . . New York and Philadel-
    phia: E. Ferrett and Co., 1845.
        W I 2695.

* Which: The Right, or the Left? New York: Garrett and
    Co., 1855.
        W II 2695.

Whittier, John Greenleaf. Legends of New England. Hart-
    ford: Hanmer and Phelps, 1831.
        W I 2710.

* Williams, Mrs. Catherine Read. Annals of the Aristoc-
    racy: Being a Series of Anecdotes of Some of the
    Principal Families of Rhode-Island. 2 nos. Provi-
    dence: B. T. Albro, printer, 1845.
        W I 2719.

_____. Religion at Home: A Story Founded on
    Facts. 2d ed. Providence: Printed by B. Cranston
    and Co., 1837.
        W I 2726.

* [Willis, Nathaniel Parker.] Inklings of Adventure.
2 vols. New York: Saunders and Otley, 1836.
W I 2736.

_____. Paul Fane; or, Parts of a Life Else
Untold. . . . New York: C. Scribner; Boston:
A. Williams and Co.; London: Sampson Low, Son and
Co., 1857.
W II 2760.

* Windle, Mary Jane. Truth and Fancy: Tales Legendary,
Historic, and Descriptive. Philadelphia: C. Sher-
man, printer, 1850.
W I 2749.

* [Wright, Caleb E.] Wyoming: A Tale. New York: Harper
and Brothers, 1845.
W I 2764.

[Yale, Mrs. Catherine.] Abbie Nott and Other Knots.
By "Katinka." Philadelphia: J. B. Lippincott and
Co., 1856.
W II 2826.

II. Other works cited

Allibone, Samuel Austin. A Critical Dictionary of
English Literature and British and American Authors,
Living and Deceased. . . . 3 vols. Philadelphia:
J. B. Lippincott Co., 1897.

Appletons' Cyclopedia of American Biography. James Grant
Wilson and John Fiske, eds. 6 vols. New York:
D. Appleton and Co., 1888-1889.

The Atlantic Monthly. Vols. I-V (1857-1860).

Baldanza, Frank. Mark Twain: An Introduction and Inter-
pretation. New York: Holt, Rinehart and Winston,
Inc., 1961.

Bartley, J. O. Teague, Shenkin and Sawney: Being an
Historical Study of the Earliest Irish, Welsh and
Scottish Characters in English Plays. Cork: Cork
University Press, 1954.

Billington, Ray Allen. The Protestant Crusade: 1800-1860.
New York: The Macmillan Co., 1938.

Blanc, Robert E. James McHenry, Playwright and Novelist.
    Philadelphia: University of Pennsylvania Press,
    1939.

Brackenridge, Hugh Henry. Modern Chivalry. Ed. Claude
    M. Newlin. New York: American Book Co., 1937.

Brownson's Quarterly Review. New series, Vols. II-VI
    (1848-1852); Third series, Vols. I-III (1853-1855);
    New York series, Vols. I-IV (1856-1859); Third New
    York series, Vols. I-III (1860-1862).

The Catholic Encyclopedia. 16 vols. New York: Robert
    Appleton Co., 1907-1914.

Charvat, William. Literary Publishing in America: 1790-
    1850. Philadelphia: University of Pennsylvania
    Press, 1959.

Cushing, William. Initials and Pseudonyms: A Dictionary
    of Literary Disguises. New York: Thomas Y. Crowell
    and Co., 1885.

_____. Initials and Pseudonyms. . . . Second
    Series. New York: Thomas Y. Crowell and Co., 1888.

David, Brother, C. S. C. American Catholic Convert
    Authors: A Bio-Bibliography. . . . Detroit: Walter
    Romig and Co., 1944.

Dictionary of American Biography. Allen Johnson, ed.
    20 vols. New York: Charles Scribner's Sons, 1928-
    1936.

Dictionary of National Biography. Leslie Stephen and
    Sidney Lee, eds. 22 vols. Reissue. New York:
    The Macmillan Co., 1908-1909.

Duyckinck, Evert A., and Duyckinck, George L., eds.
    Cyclopedia of American Literature: Embracing Per-
    sonal and Critical Notices of Authors. . . .
    Philadelphia: Wm. Rutter and Co., 1875; reprinted,
    Detroit: Gale Research Co., 1965.

Hale, Mrs. Sara Josepha. Woman's Record; or, Sketches of
    All Distinguished Women, from the Creation to
    A.D. 1854. . . . 2d ed., rev., with additions.
    New York: Harper and Brothers, 1860.

Handlin, Oscar. Boston's Immigrants: A Study in Accul-
    turation. Rev. and enl. ed. Cambridge: Harvard
University Press, 1959.

_____. The Uprooted. Boston: Little, Brown
    and Co., 1952.

Hansen, Marcus Lee. The Atlantic Migration, 1607-1860:
    A History of the Continuing Settlement of the United
    States. Ed. with foreword by A. M. Schlesinger.
    Cambridge: Harvard University Press, 1940.

Harper's New Monthly Magazine, Vols. I-XXXVI (1850-1867).

Kirk, John Foster. A Supplement to Allibone's Critical
    Dictionary of English Literature. . . . Philadel-
    phia: J. B. Lippincott Co., 1897.

Lewis, Matthew Gregory. The Monk: A Romance. . . .
    3 vols. London: J. Bell, 1796.

Littell's Living Age, Vols. I-XXXI (1844-1851).

The Official Catholic Directory. New York: P. J. Kenedy
    and Sons, annual.

Porter, David. Journal of a Cruise Made to the Pacific
    Ocean, by Captain David Porter, in the United States
    Frigate Essex. . . . 2 ed., 2 vols. New York:
    Wiley and Halsted, 1822.

Rourke, Constance. American Humor: A Study of the
    National Character. Anchor Books. New York:
    Doubleday and Co., 1953.

Thomas, Russell. "Melville's Use of Some Sources in The
    Encantadas." American Literature, III (January,
    1932), 432-456.

Thompson, George. My Life; or, The Adventures of Geo.
    Thompson: Being the Auto-Biography of an Author.
    Boston: Federhen and Co., 1854.

Thorp, Willard. American Humorists. Minneapolis: Uni-
    versity of Minnesota Press, 1964.

_____. "Catholic Novelists in Defense of their
    Faith, 1829-1865." Proceedings of the American
    Antiquarian Society, LXXV (1969), 25-117.

Tryon, Warren S., and Charvat, William. The Cost Books of Ticknor and·Fields and their Predecessors, 1832-1858. Monograph series, no. 2. New York: Bibliographical Society of America, 1949.

Whitman, Walt. The Early Poems and the Fiction. Thomas L. Brasher, ed. The Collected Writings of Walt Whitman. New York: New York University Press, 1963.

Wittke, Carl. The Irish in America. Baton Rouge: Louisiana State University Press, 1956.

Woodham-Smith, Cecil. The Great Hunger. New York: Harper and Row, 1962.

Wright, Lyle H. American Fiction, 1774-1850: A Contribution toward a Bibliography. Rev. ed. San Marino: The Huntington Library, 1948.

_____. American Fiction; 1851-1875: A Contribution toward a Bibliography. San Marino: The Huntington Library, 1957.

INDEX

Adams, Francis Colburn
Our World, 111-113, 142n

Adams, William Taylor
In Doors and Out, 50-51

The Adventures of Huckle-
berry Finn (Twain), 5-6

Afloat and Ashore (Cooper),
32n, 65, 70, 132n,
137-138

Allen, Martha
Day-Dreams, 138

Allibone, Samuel Austin
A Critical Dictionary,
22n, 23

American Fiction, 1774-1850
(Wright), 2n, 18, 19, 21

American Fiction, 1851-1875
(Wright), 2n, 18, 21

American Humor (Rourke), 63n

American Humorists (Thorp),
118

The American Lounger
(Ingraham), 61n, 90

Annals of the Aristocracy
(Williams), 67

Appletons' Cyclopedia of
American Biography, 22n

The Aristocrat (Bickley),
61n, 69n

Arthur, Timothy Shay, 18, 20,
21, 22, 49
The Home Mission, 50
The Ruined Family, 77n, 90
Sketches of Life and Char-
acter, 61n
Sparing to Spend, 76-77
What Can Woman Do?, 49-50

The Atlantic Migration
(Hansen), 162

The Atlantic Monthly, 24

Aunt Phyllis' Cabin (Eastman), 110-111

Baldanza, Frank
Mark Twain, 118n

Ballou, Maturin Murray
Roderick the Rover, 27,
142n

The Barclays of Boston (Otis),
136

Bartley, J. O.
Teague, Shenkin and Sawney,
7-10, 26n, 83

The Belle, the Blue, and the
Bigot (Tuthill), 52-53,
137, 144n, 146

Bennett, Emerson
Rosalie Dupont, 135

Bickford, Mrs. J. T.
Scandal, 55n

Bickley, Lloyd Wharton
The Aristocrat, 61n, 69n

THE IRISH-AMERICANS

An Arno Press Collection

Athearn, Robert G. **THOMAS FRANCIS MEAGHER:** An Irish Revolutionary in America. 1949

Biever, Bruce Francis. **RELIGION, CULTURE AND VALUES:** A Cross-Cultural Analysis of Motivational Factors in Native Irish and American Irish Catholicism. 1976

Bolger, Stephen Garrett. **THE IRISH CHARACTER IN AMERICAN FICTION, 1830-1860.** 1976

Browne, Henry J. **THE CATHOLIC CHURCH AND THE KNIGHTS OF LABOR.** 1949

Buckley, John Patrick. **THE NEW YORK IRISH:** Their View of American Foreign Policy, 1914-1921. 1976

Cochran, Alice Lida. **THE SAGA OF AN IRISH IMMIGRANT FAMILY:** The Descendants of John Mullanphy. 1976

Corbett, James J. **THE ROAR OF THE CROWD.** 1925

Cronin, Harry C. **EUGENE O'NEILL:** Irish and American; A Study in Cultural Context. 1976

Cuddy, Joseph Edward. **IRISH-AMERICAN AND NATIONAL ISOLATIONISM, 1914-1920.** 1976

Curley, James Michael. **I'D DO IT AGAIN:** A Record of All My Uproarious Years. 1957

Deasy, Mary. **THE HOUR OF SPRING.** 1948

Dinneen, Joseph. **WARD EIGHT.** 1936

Doyle, David Noel. **IRISH-AMERICANS, NATIVE RIGHTS AND NATIONAL EMPIRES:** The Structure, Divisions and Attitudes of the Catholic Minority in the Decade of Expansion, 1890-1901. 1976

Dunphy, Jack. **JOHN FURY.** 1946

Fanning, Charles, ed. **MR. DOOLEY AND THE CHICAGO IRISH:** An Anthology. 1976

Farrell, James T. **FATHER AND SON.** 1940

Fleming, Thomas J. **ALL GOOD MEN.** 1961

Funchion, Michael F. **CHICAGO'S IRISH NATIONALISTS, 1881-1890.** 1976

Gudelunas, William A., Jr. and William G. Shade. **BEFORE THE MOLLY MAGUIRES:** The Emergence of the Ethno-Religious Factor in the Politics of the Lower Anthracite Region, 1844-1872. 1976

Henderson, Thomas McLean. **TAMMANY HALL AND THE NEW IMMIGRANTS:** The Progressive Years. 1976

Hueston, Robert Francis. **THE CATHOLIC PRESS AND NATIVISM, 1840-1860.** 1976

Joyce, William Leonard. **EDITORS AND ETHNICITY:** A History of the Irish-American Press, 1848-1883. 1976

Larkin, Emmet. **THE HISTORICAL DIMENSIONS OF IRISH CATHOLICISM.** 1976

Lockhart, Audrey. **SOME ASPECTS OF EMIGRATION FROM IRELAND TO THE NORTH AMERICAN COLONIES BETWEEN 1660-1775.** 1976

Maguire, Edward J., ed. **REVEREND JOHN O'HANLON'S** *THE IRISH EMIGRANT'S GUIDE FOR THE UNITED STATES:* A Critical Edition with Introduction and Commentary. 1976

McCaffrey, Lawrence J., ed. **IRISH NATIONALISM AND THE AMERICAN CONTRIBUTION.** 1976

McDonald, Grace. **HISTORY OF THE IRISH IN WISCONSIN IN THE NINETEENTH CENTURY.** 1954

McManamin, Francis G. **THE AMERICAN YEARS OF JOHN BOYLE O'REILLY, 1870-1890.** 1976

McSorley, Edward. **OUR OWN KIND.** 1946

Moynihan, James H. **THE LIFE OF ARCHBISHOP JOHN IRELAND.** 1953

Niehaus, Earl F. **THE IRISH IN NEW ORLEANS, 1800-1860.** 1965

O'Grady, Joseph Patrick. **IRISH-AMERICANS AND ANGLO-AMERICAN RELATIONS, 1880-1888.** 1976

Rodechko, James Paul. **PATRICK FORD AND HIS SEARCH FOR AMERICA:** A Case Study of Irish-American Journalism, 1870-1913. 1976

Roney, Frank. **IRISH REBEL AND CALIFORNIA LABOR LEADER:** An Autobiography. Edited by Ira B. Cross. 1931

Roohan, James Edmund. **AMERICAN CATHOLICS AND THE SOCIAL QUESTION, 1865-1900.** 1976

Shannon, James. **CATHOLIC COLONIZATION ON THE WESTERN FRONTIER.** 1957

Shaw, Douglas V. **THE MAKING OF AN IMMIGRANT CITY:** Ethnic and Cultural Conflict in Jersey City, New Jersey, 1850-1877. 1976

Sylvester, Harry. **MOON GAFFNEY.** 1947

Tarpey, Marie Veronica. **THE ROLE OF JOSEPH McGARRITY IN THE STRUGGLE FOR IRISH INDEPENDENCE.** 1976

Vinyard, JoEllen McNergney. **THE IRISH ON THE URBAN FRONTIER:** Nineteenth Century Detroit. 1976

Walsh, James P., ed. **THE IRISH: AMERICA'S POLITICAL CLASS.** 1976

Weisz, Howard Ralph. **IRISH-AMERICAN AND ITALIAN-AMERICAN EDUCATIONAL VIEWS AND ACTIVITIES, 1870-1900:** A Comparison. 1976